*THE ECONOMICS OF
ZAMBIAN HUMANISM*

AFTER
MULUNGUSHI

Edited by BASTIAAN de GAAY FORTMAN

With a Foreword by
Dr KENNETH D KAUNDA
President of the Republic of Zambia

EAST AFRICAN PUBLISHING HOUSE

First published in 1969 by the
EAST AFRICAN PUBLISHING HOUSE
PO Box 30571, Uniafric House, Koinange Street, Nairobi, Kenya

Made and printed in Africa by
Printing and Packaging Corporation Ltd
PO Box 30157, Nairobi, Kenya

Contents

FOREWORD

Humanism in its classical Western sense connotes a denial of God. In order to avoid confusion it is, therefore, clearly necessary to state unequivocally that the use of the term in the Zambian context is the very opposite of this concept of Humanism. The choice of this term to describe the Zambian philosophy and way of life was a conscious decision and, indeed, the choice was made regardless of this classical meaning.

The basic premise in Zambian Humanism is that man is the centre of God's creation on earth; in the Christian tradition and indeed in that of other faiths, man is regarded as the highest expression of God's image and likeness. Indeed, the principles and ideals of the United Nations Charter and the Universal Declaration of Human Rights give clear recognition not only to man's rights and dignity but also to the central position he occupies in the universe with all his unfathomable power to gain mastery over his environment.

The startling advances made in science and technology in recent years are a testimony of human ingenuity and power which, in the final analysis, provide man with the means by which he is enabled to attain his economic and social ends.

Man's desire and urge to change his environment and to improve his economic and social conditions form one golden thread which runs through every human activity and endeavour and, indeed, through men's lives from time immemorial. Better and more improved conditions of life are the best guarantee for individual and national freedom and independence.

To improve the quality of man's life in this harsh and competitive world is not an easy task. It requires a continued reassessment and reorganisation of the development or productive machinery in the economy; it requires changes in the methods of distribution of goods and services so that the whole economic machinery is geared to meet in concrete terms the goals of economic and social action; to ensure the fair and effective flow of wealth into every Zambian home.

Humanism, therefore, as a way of life would logically imply in its practical implementation that in the final analysis Zambians must control their own economy. If they are to assert their freedom, their rights and their dignity; if they are to be self-reliant, a factor which in itself is the surest way of enhancing individual dignity and self-respect, and of increasing individual liberty, then they must be the masters of the Zambian economy. They must control the means of production and distribution provided the necessary precautions are taken against mismanagement which would be detrimental to the above objectives. Continued control of any economy by foreigners tends to impose limitations on freedom and independence and this factor is a negation of the concept of Humanism. For economics, in the final analysis, is about man; it is concerned with the deployment and utilisation of natural resources in combination with other factors of production in order to meet individual or national economic and social ends.

While Humanism will allow maximum possible participation by Zambians in the development of the economy in order to increase the flow of goods and services, it is clear that foreign investment will continue to have a great rôle to play in Zambia's development. To this end the Foreign Investment Act is to be enacted to guarantee protection for such foreign investment in Zambia. This in itself is a testimony of the Government's open-door policy in regard to participation of foreign investors in Zambia's economic growth.

What investors ought to understand is that the Zambian Government wishes them to be collaborators in Zambia's development process and not mere "fishermen" determined to maximise the yield of their investment in statistical terms regardless of the consequences to Zambia of the rather negative contribution to economic and social change. Humanism does not prevent an investor from making profit, it merely ensures the equitable distribution of the economic returns among all participants.

In practical terms, Humanism seems to offer the best approach to the building of a democratic society in a developing country. By emphasising the importance of each and every individual in society and their role in their various areas of activity, Zambians are made to feel the weight of responsibility in nation building. Humanism, therefore, helps to build in the individual a realisation that after years of foreign rule his role is being recognised both in economic and political terms in shaping the destiny of the country; and that he is, ultimately, the goal of political, economic and social action.

I believe that the concepts of economics and social change justify the Humanist approach to life for, in the final analysis, the flow of all human action has as its object the satisfaction of human ends.

The essays in this book are the work of economists and scholars who have critically examined Humanism and its implementation in various aspects of Zambia's economic and social life. The book will be of value to those who consider Humanism as a philosophy; for the essays provide food for thought. It will be invaluable to those who consider Humanism as a way of life which requires to be improved upon. It will help them to define in clearer terms the immediate and long-term goals of Zambia's economic development programme.

This publication is, therefore, welcome to both the student and the man and woman in the field engaged in implementing Humanism.

Dr K D Kaunda

1

INTRODUCTION

"People above ideology; man above institutions'
(Dr K D Kaunda, President of the
Republic of Zambia)

Zambian Humanism is both a philosophy and a way of life. As a philosophy it requires thinking; as a way of life it has to be practised. Let us first have a look at Humanism as a philosophy.

In Zambia, Humanism does not mean the same thing as in the West where it was once defined as "the belief in unbelief". Unfortunately, the Zambian philosophy was formulated in the English language. If it had been first formulated in one of the Zambian languages, the English translator would never have used the word "Humanism". When the Westerner hears this word he tends to think of a revolt against God or at least a denial of God: it is not meaningful to speak about God, so let us confine ourselves to Man. However, to the African, who probably finds less difficulty in accepting the reality of God and his sovereignty, Western Humanism is unlikely to have great appeal.

Zambian Humanism is not a theology but an anthropology and as such it takes *man* as its starting-point, but this is not to say that it denies God. With its concern for the fulness of human life and its purpose, Humanism seems to be of a more religious nature than any other political philosophy. In Zambia, Humanism means that man should remain the master of his own achievements, that he should subdue the earth instead of being subdued by it. Everything God has created is there to serve man. Money, specialisation, economic growth, ideology, all should be man's servant rather than his master. Man should remain as highly valued as he was in the tribal community. A key passage in President Kaunda's writings is the following:

"This high valuation of Man and respect for human dignity which is a legacy of our tradition should not be lost in the new Africa. However 'modern' and 'advanced' in a Western sense this young

*nation of Zambia may become, we are fiercely determined that this
humanism will not be obscured. African society has always been man-
centred. Indeed, this is as it should be, otherwise why is a house built?
Not to give man shelter and security? Why make a chair at all?
Why build a factory? Why do you want a State ranch? For what
else would there be reason to grow food? Why is the fishing industry
there? We can go on asking these questions. The simple and yet
difficult answer is "MAN". Simple in the sense that it is clear all
human activity centres around MAN. Difficult, too, because man has
not yet understood his own importance. And yet we can say with
justification and without a sense of false pride that the African way
of life with its many problems has less setbacks towards the achievement of an ideal society. We in Zambia intend to do everything in
our power to keep our society man-centred. For it is in this that what
might be described as African civilisation is embodied and indeed if
modern Africa has anything to contribute to this troubled world, it is
in this direction that it should."*

Zambian Humanism is concerned with the fulness of life; it
wants human life to be complete and attempts to fight *alienation*.
It is not based on a concept of conflict but on one of harmony.
Since for the Westerner the essence of Zambian Humanism—
namely: "MAN FOR MAN"—is not clear at first sight, let me
first try to give a Western interpretation of this anthropology of
harmony.

Essentially, man faces four basic relationships in life. In the first
place, there is a relationship with God which gives man purpose in
life and makes him realize the necessity of a choice between good
and evil, right and wrong. God has placed man under a basic
normativity so that man may know that he should love peace and
hate war, serve his fellow human beings instead of exploiting them
and use the material resources for his betterment instead of wasting
them. Secondly, man stands in a continuous relationship with his
fellow human beings. There is to be *community* in life. In this
relationship man can discover what the abstract norms of justice
and love imply. Thirdly, man has a relationship with the material
world. Material things should not be used in a chaotic way but
should be directed towards certain purposes and ultimately serve
the betterment of human life (technical efficiency, economic effectiveness). Finally, there is the relationship with himself. Man should
use the opportunities which he is given and be free to develop

himself. Life is not complete without *personality*. Each individual human being has his own potentialities and personal responsibilities. The philosophy of Humanism stresses that in all human action the *whole picture* should be kept in mind and not one relationship emphasised to the exclusion of the other relationships. In employing his labour, land and capital, for example, man should not only strive for technical and economic efficiency but also for justice in the community. A *man-centred society* is a society in which there is a continuous striving for *full* human life. Life should never be reduced to a number of material ends, nor just to community, nor just to personality.

For most readers the foregoing will probably be heavy stuff. If they are Westerners they are likely to have—as President Kaunda once pointed out—a "problem solving" mind, as opposed to the "situation experiencing" mind of the African. The question they want to ask is probably: "How can Humanism solve the problems of the Zambian economy?" In this book that question is not neglected. But at this point it may be good to emphasise that Zambian Humanism is a philosophy and that as such it requires some independent thinking on the part of those who want to understand it. It is, as President Kaunda has said, "something that is going to be very difficult for a foreigner to understand properly".

Zambian Humanism is not an ideology in the sense of a given set of ideas which enable people to interpret life without thinking. This is an important point. Humanism cannot simply be imitated, it has to be understood. From the Zambians it demands that they look into their own society and think about how the dangers of an "invading money-economy" should be faced.

Thus Humanism can lead to political unity in Zambia only if the individual Zambians when they think about the development of their society come to the same conclusions. Of course much can be taught to them—for example how a modern money-economy works and to what sorts of unhappiness it has led in the countries it invaded. But if they do not feel these dangers are *real dangers* and if they do not think certain values of traditional societies in Zambia have to be preserved, then Humanism will remain a philosophy but never become the Zambian way of life.

*   *   *

Perhaps the most interesting cultural question today is whether the whole world is going to modernise and whether this necessarily implies that the whole world is going to Westernise or even to Americanise. Just as Europeans deny that Americanisation is inevitable, Zambians believe they can avoid Westernisation. "I am deeply concerned," President Kaunda wrote to Colin Morris, "that [the] high valuation of Man and respect for human dignity, which is a legacy of our tradition, should not be lost in the new Africa. However 'modern' and 'advanced' in a Western sense the new nations of Africa may become, we are fiercely determined that this humanism will not be obscured. African society has always been Man-centred. We intend that it will remain so."

The Westerner tends to look at these Humanist ideals with a certain amount of cynicism. To him it seems inevitable that Zambia is going to face the same problems of materialism, of exploitation, group egotism and class conflicts that the West has experienced and still experiences. To President Kaunda's plaintive question: "Is there any way that my people can have the blessing of technology without being eaten away by materialism and losing the spiritual dimension from their lives?" the Westerner will simply answer: "No, there is not!" President Kaunda's answer, however, is not simply "Yes, there is!" He says: "I suppose the answer is that however intensely we industrialise, the vast majority of the peoples of Africa will still live in close contact with Nature and so keep alive this element in our culture." We may take this answer as *conditional*. If Zambia opts for the Western ambitions which can be stated in terms of production and consumption and are to be attained through rigorous self-advancement or collective advancement by the State, then it will not escape the *alienation* that is inherent in the Western type of society whether it be capitalist or socialist. If money should be man's servant rather than his master, its rôle in the development of the country is to be limited. In other words, Zambia would have to adopt policies and create checks and balances which aim at preserving a "humanist way of life" and for that purpose it should be prepared to accept a lower growth rate of the national income *per capita* than would otherwise be possible.

African leaders who state that they want to preserve certain values of the tribal community tend to be greeted with remarks about their "naïvety". Let me emphasise, therefore, that President Kaunda is well aware that with the impact of the money economy the Zambian mutual aid society can never be the same again. Nor does he pretend that the traditional tribal society was a perfect *mutual aid society* and a completely *accepting* and *inclusive community*. But these were the accepted ideals and there was a great deal of striving towards the ideals. It is the President's hope that a mutual aid society, an accepting community and an inclusive community will remain the *ideals* in modern Zambia and that there will be intensive efforts to attain these ideals.

The formulation of policies which aim, in the first place, at improving the *quality* of people's life, and the creation of checks and balances on "unhumanist" actions, present of course tremendous problems. In this book some of these problems are analysed.

* * *

It is worthy of note that Zambian politics are primarily concerned with the problem of harmonious development. If Zambian politics were pervaded by polemics with the white minority regimes in southern Africa, nobody would be surprised. But although Zambia is quite outspoken on this point it does not allow its own politics to be dominated by polemics or rancour. It should also be noted that Zambia with its 80,000 whites, knows what it is talking about when it rejects the Western type of society. It has a Western society in its own country and in fact a very rich and happy one. Northern Rhodesia was a white man's paradise. Since Dumont's "*L'Afrique noire est mal partie*" (False start in Africa) there is a lot of talk about African elites which want to imitate the old colonialists. It is amazing however—certainly from the Western point of view— that this desire to lead a white man's life is not more widespread. African leaders such as Dr. Kaunda have not forgotten that the same society which internally was so rich and happy, was able to reject the African as a fellow human being with equal rights and responsibilities.

Humanism as a *way of life* is modelled on the *mutual aid society*. This society finds its basis in the tribal community in which "human need was the supreme criterion of behaviour" and where "social harmony was a vital necessity . . . [since] every activity was a matter of teamwork." The majority of the Zambian people still live in this type of community. Humanism aims at improving the quality of these people's lives which clearly also demands an improvement in their material conditions. The challenge is to preserve a mutual aid society when such a society is no longer a matter of life and death. And the key phrase in meeting this challenge is "development from below" or, as the Tanzanians say, "self-reliance".

It may be interesting to note that the *mutual aid society* is becoming an ideal in the West too. But there the ideal is derived not from the past but from the future. In a completely cybernetised economy in which only two per cent of the population have to work in the production system—as controllers of the controlling machines— everybody can receive a guaranteed income from the community as a whole, and then live a full life, free from the domination of the profit motive (see, for example, R. Theobald's *The Guaranteed Income*). I do not think that this cultural-economic ideal is less far removed from the present-day Western society than Humanism is from present-day Zambian society. The difference is noteworthy. The Western ideal demands a faster rate of technological change and in consequence probably a faster rate of alienation before the great day should come when the ideal society can be formed. The Zambian ideal demands a cautious and harmonious absorption of technological change. In Europe progressive people do not talk about preserving certain values of the past; in Africa they do. The obvious advantage a country like Zambia has, as compared with many Western countries, is that it has not as yet become alienated from its own past. It is understandable that Zambia wants to preserve its tie with the past.

★   ★   ★

This book is intended for both Zambians and interested people outside Zambia. It sets out to confront Zambians with some cold facts and sober problems which demand the formulation of concrete policies. The African mind, according to President Kaunda, tends to think in terms of *both–and* as opposed to the Western mind which thinks in terms of *either–or*. Dr. Kaunda admits, however, that problems exist which are not susceptible of a *both–and* approach but which require that choices be made. The members of the Economics Department of the University of Zambia who have contributed to this book—afflicted with a *problem–solving* mind as they are—have concentrated their attention on the problems of the Zambian economy and on the need for definite policies. President

Kaunda's speech at Mulungushi* on "Zambia towards Economic Independence" is a clear policy statement and as such is a good starting point for discussing the economics of Zambian Humanism.

Thus academic economists discuss whether Humanism can answer their questions of a practical economic nature. It should be noted, however, that Humanism in its turn poses the academic economist with certain questions. Humanism demands a commitment towards the development of *each one* of the four million inhabitants of Zambia. Have economists anything to contribute here or are they merely concerned with the macroeconomic problem of growth of real national income? Do they think at all about the relationship between economics and human relations?

The basis of this collection consists in the ideas of Zambians on the development of their own country, and should therefore be of interest to those people outside Zambia who wish to know more about Zambian Humanism and its rôle in the development of the country. It opens with President Kaunda's basic documents on Zambian Humanism and its importance for the development of the Zambian economy: "Humanism in Zambia" and "Zambia Towards Economic Independence". When studying these papers the reader will discover that Humanism is intended to arm the nation *for* the challenge of development and *against* the dangers of "an invading money-economy". In a penetrating contribution, Dr. J. B. Zulu, Governor of the Bank of Zambia, further elaborates on the confrontation between Humanism and money.

The Editor's article, "Humanism and the Zambian Economic Order", analyses in a general way how Zambia through its philosophy of Humanism and the related policies of controlled private enterprise, development from below, and economic co-operation, is attempting to commit all the nation's resources towards the development of its subsistence economy. A more detailed discussion of the problems and policies concerning Zambia's agrarian revolution is provided by Dr. Charles Elliott in his contribution on Humanism and agriculture in Zambia.

A developing country like Zambia, with a fairly advanced money-economy and a subsistence economy within the same borders, is frequently faced with the problem of "workers exploiting peasants".

---

*Mulungushi, the birthplace of Zambia's independence, is about 100 miles north of Lusaka. Here the ruling United National Independence Party generally holds its big political meetings.

Father Kevin Quinn, s.j. deals with this important subject in his essay on Humanism and labour.

Dr. N. A. Mujumdar writes on the implications of the new economic policy for the banking and monetary sectors. He proposes a credit policy which would fight inflation and at the same time promote Zambian entrepreneurship. Stephen H. Goodman discusses Zambian investment policy. Obviously the question of how best to use the country's limited investment opportunities is of major importance for Zambia's development.

The book concludes with an address by President Kaunda in which he urges non-Zambians to try and understand Zambian Humanism and the policies formulated in Mulungushi.

On finishing the book the reader will doubtless feel that many questions remain unanswered. This is inevitable. But if this symposium has in some way helped to stimulate wider discussion of the economics of Zambian Humanism, we shall feel that our main purpose has been achieved.

BASTIAAN DE GAAY FORTMAN

The University of Zambia
August 1968

2

HUMANISM IN ZAMBIA*

His Excellency Dr K D Kaunda
President of the Republic of Zambia

PREAMBLE

The art of colonisation, if it is to succeed, means a coloniser sees to it that the victim is not only colonised politically, but also economically and culturally. This being the case, the act of political independence forms but the first part of the process of decolonisation. This process is a very long one.

Perhaps it is not possible to complete it in one generation, for it does not only require careful thought and planning, but also a lot of material, human and otherwise, to bring it about.

In many ways it is even more difficult than the attainment of political independence. All the same, time does come for the leaders of any given revolution, if they know what they are doing, to think of starting to remould their society.

For only by so doing would they profit from the wisdom and values of their forefathers.

Of course, it would be wrong to do this with closed minds, for while there is plenty of good that Africa is justly proud of in its set-up of a mutual aid society—a society in which people worked co-operatively and collectively without losing the identity of the individual for whose benefit and in whose name all was done— one has got to understand and appreciate that the powerful forces from the West which have been aggressively shattering in their individualistic, competitive and possessive approach, have had serious and grave consequences on the African society.

Indeed, even the good side of life from the West has had its own

*Pamphlet prepared for the National Council of the United National Independence Party at Lusaka, 26th April, 1967.

effects on the African society which we can only ignore at our own peril. One can think of science and technology and health facilities which are fast increasing Africa's population, after the devastating slave trade. One can think, too, of the industrialisation process, modern agricultural techniques as well as all other complexities brought about in the wake of these contacts with the West.

Now during the hazardous road to political independence, we recognised the fact that Africa was going to be one of the biggest, if not the biggest, battleground for this century's ideological battles. As is well known, the present-day ideological differences are based on certain economic and political theories and practices. Putting it very simply, one would say it was a question of who owned or controlled the means of creating and distributing wealth in any given nation.

In other words, is it the State or individuals who are to own the means of creating wealth, or is it both, and if it is both, in what proportions? After this, how fair is the distribution of this wealth and, indeed, what methods are used to distribute it in any given nation?

This is a key point, for if the distribution of wealth is not done properly, it might lead to the creation of classes in society and the much-valued humanist approach that is traditional and inherent in our African society would have suffered a final blow. If this happened the world as a whole, and Africa in particular, would be all the poorer by it. For you would then have the "haves" and the "have-nots". Politically you would be creating room for opposing parties based on "the oppressed" and "the oppressor" concept which again would not be in keeping with the society described above: a society in which the Chief as an elected or appointed leader of the people held national property like land in trust for the people, and he was fully aware that he was responsible to them. He knew, too, that his continuing to be their head depended on his people's will.

The African society was progressive and human. The present generation with its responsibilities of taking care of the past traditions, remoulding the present to prepare for future generations, would do well to bear this in mind in all its political, economic, social and cultural activities.

The question we must now address ourselves to is, in what respect and how much will it be necessary to change our traditional

African society and reconstruct it as it emerges from a non-money to a money status. We will have to take into consideration the impact the use of money has made on our society. Economists will tell us that the use of money presupposes exchange and exchange presupposes specialisation and these three are inseparably linked in a self-generating process. It is a well-known fact that as the money economy expands, such as it is fast doing in Zambia, Government is being forced to push people to become more and more specialised in various fields; and as the people become more and more specialised, they are becoming more and more effective in their fields and, all other factors being equal, the money economy will expand.

Now we must ask again what effects will persistently increasing levels of specialisation have on our much-valued traditional society in our country. This field of specialisation drives people to resort to new groups in society. In other words, people with common interests group together, paitly because of the community of their interests and partly as the means of promoting and protecting the welfare of their group. For example, a carpenter will find his own interests are not the same as those of the plasterer. The factory worker finds that his interests differ from those of the commercial farmer. The teacher finds that his interests differ from those of the mineworker. And so the whole list of different interests can be outlined. The point is, all this gives birth to a new disintegrative tendency. This, as can be seen, cuts right across the traditional society which has been described above as a mutual aid society which was an accepting and inclusive community.

What has been outlined in our immediately preceding paragraphs shows clearly that we will have to find answers as time goes on to the following points:

(1) in what respect the advent of a money economy will result in changes in the traditional society and social structure;

(2) whether it is desirable that these structural changes be checked either in part or in full, and, if so,

(3) whether it is possible through policies implemented by Government to impose the desired checks without also checking the growth of specialisation and of material wealth for our people.

Finally, the introductory part must end with a warning. Whatever changes take place in our society, whatever sacrifices are made or are urged on individuals to make, by the Party and Government, in our task of fighting to preserve the Man-centred society, we must remember that it is people above ideology; Man above institutions. We must continuously refuse to slavishly tie men to anything. Society is there because of Man. We choose the hard way of continually experimenting on our generally agreed path, ready to learn from anyone from any part of the world according to our agreed principles. In other words, whatever we undertake to do we have got to remember that it is Man that is the centre of all human activity.

Chapter I
ZAMBIAN IDEOLOGY IS HUMANISM
Part One

In its task of defining Humanism the Party will obviously have to be guided first by what it has declared it believes in, and secondly, by what it has done in the last three years of independence—action and not just fine words. Thirdly, our Humanism must be understood against the background of what we know to have been the way of life enjoyed by our forefathers. We must begin now with an analysis of the type of society enjoyed by them.

Part Two

Let us deal with the third point in Part One first. There is no doubt at all that the greatest blessing bestowed on Africa, if one can generalise, is that we have always had a gift for man enjoying the fellowship of man simply because he is man. This is at the heart of our traditional culture. With the advent of independence the possibility exists of extending the scale of our discovery by example to the rest of the world.

We have held, and we still hold, that Africa's gift to world culture must be in the field of Human Relations. It might be mentioned in passing, therefore, that to this extent we have talked of establishing a chair in Human Relations as against just race relations, at the University of Zambia. Human Relations is a subject much wider in its coverage than the latter.

The traditional community was a mutual aid society. It was organised to satisfy the basic human needs of all its members and, therefore, individualism was discouraged. Most resources, such as land, might be communally owned and administered by chiefs and village headmen for the benefit of everyone. If, for example, a villager required a new hut, all the men would turn to forests and fetch poles to erect the frame and bring grass for thatching. The women might be responsible for making the mud-plaster for the walls and two or three of them would undoubtedly brew some beer so that all the workers would be refreshed after a hot but satisfying day's work. In the same spirit, the able-bodied would accept responsibility for tending and harvesting the gardens of the sick and infirm.

Human need was the supreme criterion of behaviour. The hungry stranger could, without penalty, enter the garden of a village and take, say, some peanuts, a bunch of bananas, a mealie cob or a cassava plant root to satisfy his hunger. His action only became theft if he took more than was necessary to satisfy his needs. For then he was depriving others.

Obviously, social harmony was a vital necessity in such a community where almost every activity was a matter of teamwork. Hence, chiefs and traditional elders had an important judicial and reconciliatory function. They adjudicated between conflicting parties, admonished the quarrelsome and anti-social and took whatever action was necessary to strengthen the fabric of social life. Mention must be made here of the fact that when any of these anti-social activities were punished, very often the punishment was heavy. It should be emphasised that this way of life was not a kind of idealised social experiment such as may be found in Europe where groups of people take themselves off into pleasant rural surroundings in order to avoid the tensions of industrial society. Life in the bush is hard and dangerous and a high degree of social cohesion is necessary for survival. The basic unit of life is not the individual or immediate family (as in industrial societies) but the community. This means that there must be fundamental agreement upon goals and all must act together.

For example, when a marauding lion attacked, the menfolk went out to hunt the dangerous killer. Now the spirit of social cohesion was so much developed that those who went out had only their community at heart and not their individual lives. The results were spectacular.

In the second place, the traditional community was an accepting community. It did not take account of failure in an absolute sense. The slow, the inept and incapable were accepted as any other member in community life provided they were socially amenable. Social qualities weighed much heavier in the balance than individual achievement. The success–failure complex seems to be a disease of the age of individualism—the result of a society conditioned by the diploma, the examination and the selection procedure. In the best tribal society people were valued not for what they could achieve but because they were there. Their contribution, however limited, to the material welfare of the village was acceptable, but it was their presence not their achievement which was appreciated.

Take, for instance, the traditional African attitude to old people. Here it should be pointed out how horrified an African is, in most cases, on the first occasion of his acquaintance with the Western phenomenon of old people's homes. The idea that the State or some voluntary agency should care for the aged was anathema to Africa, for it almost seems to imply that old people are a nuisance who must be kept out of the way so that children can live their lives unhampered by their presence. In traditional societies, old people are venerated and it is regarded as a privilege to look after them. Their counsel is sought on many matters and, however infirm they might be, they have a valued and constructive rôle to play in teaching and instructing their grandchildren. Indeed, to deny a grandparent the joy of the company of his grandchildren is a heinous sin. The fact that old people can no longer work, or are not as alert as they used to be, or even have developed the handicaps of senility in no way affects our regard for them. We cannot do enough to repay them for all they have done for us. They are the embodiment of wisdom; living symbols of our continuity with the past.

No doubt a defender of the Western and Eastern ways of life might retort that institutions for the care of old people are inevitable in large-scale societies and that but for the efforts of the State and voluntary agencies many old people would starve. This is undoubtedly true, but it merely serves to underline the point that in a society which regards person-to-person relationships as supremely important no one can be so isolated that responsibility for his welfare cannot be determined and assigned.

The experts have all kinds of standards by which they judge the degree of civilisation of a people. In the African traditional society the test is this. How does that society treat its old people and, indeed, all its members who are not useful and productive in the narrowest sense? Judged by this standard, the so-called advanced societies have a lot to learn which the so-called backward societies could teach them.

In the third place, the traditional community was an inclusive society. In other words, the web of relationships which involved some degree of mutual responsibility was widely spread. One could describe industrial society as an exclusive society because its members' responsibilities are often confined to the immediate family, and it may be noted that the family circle may be a self-entire little universe, preventing the acceptance of wider commitments.

Here is an example of the inclusiveness of the traditional society. An African does not restrict the title "father" to his male parent. He also addresses his father's brothers as "father". And he calls his mother's sisters "mother" also. Only his father's sisters would be addressed as "aunt" and his mother's brothers as "uncle". "Brothers" would include not only the male children of his father but also certain cousins and even members of the same clan who have no blood relationship in the Western sense. Now, to the Western mind, this confusing state of affairs is not merely a matter of terminology. These are not just courtesy titles. With the title "father", for example, goes all the responsibility of parenthood and in return all the "fathers" receive filial devotion. Hence, no child in a traditional society is likely to be orphaned. Should his literal parents die then others automatically assume the responsibility for his upbringing. By the same token no old person is likely to end his days outside a family circle. If his own offspring cannot care for him then other "children" will accept the duty and privilege.

The extended family system constitutes a social security scheme which has the advantage of following the natural pattern of personal relationships rather than being the responsibility of an institution. It also provides for richness in knowledge and experience for those fortunate enough to be part of it. Granted, the characteristics of small-scale societies have been described and it could be argued that such a system would not work where hundreds of thousands of people are gathered together in cities and towns. But the attitudes to human beings as described above are not solely a function of social organisation. They are now part of the African psychology.

This high valuation of MAN and respect for human dignity which is a legacy of our tradition should not be lost in the new Africa. However "modern" and "advanced" in a Western sense this young nation of Zambia may become, we are fiercely determined that this humanism will not be obscured. African society has always been man-centred. Indeed, this is as it should be otherwise why is a house built? Not to give man shelter and security? Why make a chair at all? Why build a factory? Why do you want a State ranch? For what else would there be need to grow food? Why is the fishing industry there? We can go on asking these questions. The simple and yet difficult answer is "MAN". Simple in the sense that it is clear all human activity centres around MAN. Difficult, too, because man has not yet understood his own importance. And yet we can say with justification and without any sense of false pride that the African way of life with its many problems has less setbacks towards the achievement of an ideal society. We in Zambia intend to do everything in our power to keep our society man-centred. For it is in this that what might be described as African civilisation is embodied and indeed if modern Africa has anything to contribute to this troubled world, it is in this direction that it should.

From this definition a number of questions must be asked. With so many forces at work in Africa as a whole, and in Zambia in particular, how can a system of this type, which is really principally based on mutual trust within members of that society, survive? For is it not clear that both the East and the West do not subscribe to this way of life either by design or by sheer force of circumstances in which they operate? Indeed, all white minority Governments round Zambia do not subscribe to this philosophy either. For example, the social security of an individual in our traditional society was based on the understanding that this was a mutual aid society. How does an individual in Zambia today remain mutual-aid-society-minded and at the same time function in a society that is emerging from a so-called modern economy which has been born out of capitalism? On the other hand, how does he meet this challenge without going to the excesses of the ultra-left where man is equally "dehumanised"—and remains more as an instrument rather than the master of institutions? These questions must be answered as we map out our path for, as a young, vigorous, and forward-looking nation, we will need to spell out clearly how we go about this.

Now and in future

One has strong fears that although leaders preached the importance of man before independence and have continued to do so after it, this and its true meaning has not begun to permeate the rank and file of the Party, Civil Service, the Police, our Army and the general public to any appreciable extent. The question is how can we begin to inject this into the bloodstream of the nation?

The fact that (and this is not, repeat not, to glorify the past but rather to humbly try to learn from it for the good of the present and the future) our ancestors were able to achieve a society in which social and political order was tight and effective calls for some examination on our part of how they have achieved this.

This, of course, did not come about by making high sounding declarations in the form of ideologies, etc. It came about by a carefully worked out order and discipline which everybody in society was required to follow. The teaching of their own values and the imparting of knowledge and wisdom by the elders to the youth of the community was part and parcel of this carefully worked out order and discipline. So that we see that the elders in the community used each day very carefully. Early in the morning they would rise to go either cultivating, hunting or fishing; if they were a cattle-rearing people—grazing cattle; or any other economic activities. In the evenings they would pool their experiences of the day while at their communal eating places or, indeed, as was often the case, while beer would be taken, which was strictly speaking an affair for the old people, while the young men sat around deeply interested in the knowledge and wisdom that was being imparted, knowing only too well that tomorrow it would be their turn. Is this social harmony still possible? Frankly, the answer is "Yes"; it is a question of how we organise society in the face of those shattering and aggressive forces already referred to (from both the West and the East).

From what has been said above, it is clear that we cannot ourselves expect to achieve once again the Man-centred society without very careful planning. And in this direction nothing is more important than institutions of learning. These must be given a wider definition than what we might loosely refer to as the conventional. In other words, emphasis must be laid on the preventive rather than on the curative side of life, if we are to avoid the pitfalls experienced by other people. Here one is not only obliged to think of boys and girls from Grade I, to the University of Zambia students, but also of all institutions, that is, teacher training colleges, trades and technical schools and any other institution where any form of teaching or instruction is carried out, whether it be in Government or in private hands. Our leading educationalists, sociologists and psychologists ought to be able to work out a curriculum that would become part and parcel of all that was being taught wherever any form of instruction were being given.

Our much-talked-about Department of Human Relations at the University of Zambia would then act at a national level as a sort of watchdog, to see how we were faring in this direction, while at the international level it continued to explore the possibilities of better understanding within the community of nations. It is said that a newly wedded couple guard each other jealously against intruders from outside. This is even more so in the case of Parties and Governments that lead newly independent countries like Zambia. In spite of this, care must be taken that we do not overstress or over-emphasise the importance of preserving our past society at the expense of the material development of our people. This, in fact, is the crucial point: how do we preserve what is good in our traditions and at the same time allow ourselves to benefit from the science and the technology of our friends from both the West and the East. We refuse to be dogmatic about anything. That is, this Party and Government is not given to the art of drawing fixed lines somewhere between any two end-choices. We choose to be constantly looking for and devising new ways by which to encourage the hastening of material advance while ensuring that the principles of traditional Man-centred society are preserved.

*   *   *

The achieving of African democratic socialism for Northern Rhodesia was in Clause (l) in the Party's pre-Independence con-stitution* and in the post-Independence Constitution† this becomes point number one in our aims and objects. It is obvious, therefore, that the attainment of a socialist society in our country has been

---

*"To achieve African Democratic Socialism for Northern Rhodesia, raise the standard of living of the people and generally make the people of Northern Rhodesia contented and happy people."

†"To achieve African Democratic Socialism for Zambia, raise the standard of living of the people and generally strive to make the people of Zambia contented and happy."

cardinal in all our thinking and activities. It must be emphasised that this is not a new thing in our society. This, of course, has partly been shown above.

By advocating a humanist way of life we are appreciating the wisdom and values of our forefathers. Mere appreciation, however, of a good thing is not sufficient even if it is written down. What is required is understanding the philosophy and appreciating the importance of methods of organisation, that is, organising for a humanist society.

Those of us who have read Christian history will know that the gospel might not have survived the onslaught of the ancient Jews, Romans, barbarians and others had it not won over to itself powerful exponents and organisers such as St. Paul, St. Peter and others.

The next question we must deal with now is the second in Part One, How far have we gone in the direction of attaining humanism in Zambia? To understand this let us outline precisely what this means in political, economic, social and cultural terms. Zambia can say with pride that its humanism is original, based very much on the importance of Man. In this case the State cares for Man, the Person. He, in return, as an individual will, or at least is expected to, care for his neighbour and thereby care for the State. The oft-declared principles of non-tribalism, non-racialism, no discrimination based on religion and creed is very much part of the principles embodied in the importance of the Common Man.

Now what does this humanism mean economically? Obviously, a number of questions to which we must give answers must be asked here in order to define it in understandable terms. First of all, take the means of producing wealth:

(a) Who shall own the means of producing wealth?

(b) What shall be the means?

(c) What wealth shall be produced first? (That is, we need a priority list in view of the scarcity of the resources.)

(d) Once acquired, how and who distributes this wealth?

It should be pointed out that not even the most capitalist Government can today afford to leave their country's economy entirely in private hands. Even they are at best working out tax or legislative measures to see that some, if not much more, control of their country's economy is in Government hands. On the other hand, even the most ultra-left Governments are allowing private enterprise to continue, especially in areas where Government may not have the know-how.

African humanists, therefore, if one might again generalise, can be justly proud of their understanding and definition of socialism. Zambia can proudly speak of her achievements in the last two and a half years of independence. Admittedly, much more remains to be done, but what is about to be outlined shows clearly how Zambia has answered and how she intends to answer some of those questions she has not yet already given answers to in the list of questions posed above.

Needless to point out here that to produce anything at all we need land, capital and labour. Some people might add rent to this, and perhaps for the sake of the present analysis we might add it to this list. How much of each of the three points above you need to be successful in any undertaking depends on what you want to do, to achieve, and how.

Let us now define each one of these major factors as we see them in Zambia. But before that, let us remind ourselves of what was pointed out in both the preamble and Chapter I on these three important factors. There is no doubt at all that the mutual aid society way of life is peculiarly African both in origin and pattern. Be this as it may, it borders on the one hand on capitalism, and on the other on communism.

Just to recap, our ancestors worked collectively and co-operatively from start to finish. One might say this was a communist way of doing things and yet these gardens remained strongly the property of individuals. One might say here that this was capitalism. Collectively and co-operatively they harvested but when it came to storing and selling their produce they became strongly individualistic. They did not finish at that. When it came to sharing the fruits of their labour like meals, for instance, they shared them communally. Indeed, one is compelled to say a strange mixture of nineteenth-century capitalism with communism. Yet, as is said above, this was original and the pattern essentially African.

This is what makes us realise the importance attached to Man in that society. All was done for the good of Man as a Person. It could be done collectively, it could be held individually—Man was central. Hence the strange mixture which gives the present generation the right to claim that our socialism is humanism.

Chapter II

LAND

Land, obviously, must remain the property of the State today. This in no way departs from our heritage. Land was never bought. It came to belong to individuals through usage and the passing of time. Even then the chief and the elders had overall control although, as is already pointed out, this was done on behalf of all the people.

On the other hand, Zambia's birth has come at a time when some of our fellow-men founded homes here through a capitalist system or capitalist governments. These have bought some land. It is their way of life. As is clear, we do not necessarily agree with it.

This affects us in two ways. The first is the human side of it and the second is the impact of what might be termed the price tag system of our society.

As regards the first point, we as a Government have promised that this State will not interfere with the property of individuals and we cannot go back on this at all unless, of course, as has been provided in the law of the land, this land property was not being exploited. What we can never agree to here is absentee landlordism.

The next problem is even more complicated. It is the price tag phenomenon. This price tag phenomenon means today that unlike our people working in their gardens collectively and co-operatively and still contributing to the maximum, the price tag has destroyed this in us. (One can argue, of course, that even where collective and co-operative working was concerned, the price tag was still visible in the sense that each one of those who worked on any garden or at a house, had, at the back of their own mind, that the whole group with them there would be working at their house or garden the following day or so. This in itself could be described as a price tag approach. All the same, this could not be as strong as in a money economy.)

What this means is that individual possession of land has become much more attractive to many people in our society. It can, however, be pointed out correctly that the price tag can be taken care of by making many other useful approaches to this problem in so far as working the land usefully and productively is concerned.

It is true to say that once people realised that no one would tamper with their land for years and years to come they would feel that certain. In other words, the incentive to develop to the full would not be there. One feels strongly, however, that land cannot be made and does not grow. From this one hopes the sacredness our ancestors attached to it (that is land)—so much so that they could not think of selling or buying it—will be understood and appreciated. It is, after all, the greatest material gift to man from God. When you come to think of it, it is a source of man's life and its sacredness can only continue to be if all of it is held by the State for the good of all.

In Zambia, of course, there is little land hunger, and wherever it has appeared as a result of malpractices on the part of past governments, it is fast being remedied by the people's Government.

Realising this value of land and the complications that would arise out of a much required drastic change in our present system, this Government exactly a month after Independence, on 24th November, 1964, decided that a Land Commission be appointed to inquire into the question of land tenure in Zambia. In addition, a Cabinet Land Policy Committee was also constituted with the then Minister of Lands and Natural Resources as Chairman.

Both the Cabinet Committee and the Commission have since been engaged in collating data and reviewing all aspects of the land policy which was inherited on Independence and will later submit recommendations on a comprehensive land policy. During all this period the Commission has interviewed Provincial Land Committees established in every province except Barotse, where investigations are going on at another level.

Because the task is so heavy, instead of reporting by the end of 1965, the Commission is still working. I am, however, glad to say that they will report to Government next month on their findings.

But we, as a Party, have made it absolutely clear, and the Commission is working along the lines, that land reform must be a means to greater productivity and higher standards of living for the people whose livelihood is derived from the land.

Some of you might say it has taken the Commission far too long to conclude its task. We must all be aware of the complexity of this type of work and what is involved, especially when it is realised that we have such a variety of lands here—State land, customary land—which are classified under various categories.

The Party, and indeed the whole country, knows that official approach such as it was in the colonial days believed in a policy of *laissez faire* in accordance with the hallowed principles of Indirect

Rule. Most important of all there was very little appreciation of the views of the emergent Zambian (then African) entrepreneur and farmer classes. This policy meant immense progress on what is now known as state land while it spelt misery in customary land. It is a known fact that the line of rail was not the only agriculturally deserving part of Zambia. The question of development in the rural areas has, of course, got to be looked at through the mirror of development in general for the whole country. But as land is our greatest asset and one of the factors of production, the Party must endeavour to make it play its rightful part in the sphere of national development.

Chapter III

INDUSTRIAL AND AGRICULTURAL DEVELOPMENT

Having considered briefly the question of land we might now go on to deal with industrial and agricultural development. It is clear to all of us, that ever since we took over we have been working hard to change from a capitalist system to a socialist one. It must be emphasised once again that this can never be a seven-day-wonder job. Capitalism has been entrenched in this country whether you look at it from an economic, sociological, cultural or, indeed, political angle. This statement of fact can best be illustrated by outlining what has been done, what is being done and what we intend to do in various spheres of industrial and agricultural activity in future.

Industrial and commercial

First of all, Government has clearly outlined, in keeping with the Party manifesto, the areas of economic activity in the following manner:

A. Where only Government will participate.

B. Areas where Government will participate with another Government.

C. Areas where Government will participate with another Government and private enterprise.

D. Areas where Government will participate with private enterprise and by mutual agreement Government may take over full control at a later stage.

E. Areas where co-operatives will operate with or without Government participation.

F. Those areas where Government will participate with private enterprise.

G. Those areas where only private enterprise might participate.

The following might serve as good examples of what is meant in A, B, C, D, E, F and G above:

A. Industries such as integrated iron and steel, fertilisers, arms and ammunition, public utilities such as public airways, public railways, power, water, telecommunications, wholesale outlets for general goods, wholesale outlets for building materials, development financing and banking, and, as already indicated, any other industry which Government considered to be in the national interest to promote.

A/1. State Insurance (Commercial).

B. Oil pipeline between Zambian and Tanzanian Governments.

C. Tanzam Road Service.

D. Mining development, cement, building materials, sugar, textiles, tannery, international hotels, fibre bags and sacks, and any other industry which the Government considered to be in the national interest to promote in co-operation with private enterprise.

E. This will be determined as time goes on.

F. Mining development, sugar, salt, glazed pipe and brick manufacture and explosives.

G. Mining and any other industry which Government felt should be open to private investors, both domestic and foreign.

Agricultural

Government is here again determined to fulfil the Party's promises to the country. The objective is to make the agricultural sector as productive and as profitable as the mining industry—only more permanent. To this extent, it is the intention to carry out the agrarian revolution to the best of our ability by making every village in Zambia and every individual in it productive on the land, as well as in secondary industries based on agriculture.

In this respect there will be again, as in industries, participation by—

A. Government;
B. Co-operatives (various types);
C. Private enterprise;
D. Ordinary village units which may or may not be co-operatively worked.

To give examples:—

A. 1. State ranches.
   2. State farms around which might be developed co-operative units which eventually might take over State farms. In some cases State farms are intended to continue with their own production and will also continue to be the pivot of development in those areas by helping new farms and unions of co-operatives around them with some sort of extension services.
   3. State farms used as demonstration centres.
B. 1. Co-operative farms collectively worked.
   2. Co-operative farms individually worked but marketing done co-operatively and where in some cases equipment might be bought and owned jointly.

While dealing with the issue of co-operatives it should be pointed out that in many ways the development of humanism in Zambia will depend on how successful we are in organising people's co-operatives. We must avoid the pitfalls into which others have fallen. We must never allow co-operatives to grow into just another group of exploiters. Co-operators have got to work themselves and not to employ other people.

On the other hand, Government itself must avoid putting the needs of the favoured few before the needs of the common man. We must always, repeat always, be on the lookout. This tends to be a general weakness in many developing nations. Development can only spread through the co-operative movement successfully in this State if co-operatives are truly people's co-operatives.

C. Here we are dealing with the group we call today commercial farmers who no doubt have an important rôle to play in the realisation of our agrarian revolution.
D. Villages will be organised to form productivity councils and the Party will, as it must on the co-operative side, have to

play a very important rôle, for without it we cannot succeed in these two fields. To do this the Party must give itself a new direction and a new rôle in the affairs of the country. The Regional, Political and Economic Committees are doing exceedingly well already in some provinces; in others not so well and in some they are non-existent.

It is a sad legacy that we have inherited and which should be remedied as quickly as possible, that the poorest of the poor, that is the villager, or the peasant, suffers most in terms of cost of living. If it were not for the fact that our people grow their own food we would have been in trouble already. What is required now is to organise ourselves in such a way that Government, through the Zambia National Wholesale Corporation, should help stamp out the sad exploitation of the peasant paying twice as much for what a worker in town gets more cheaply. *This is important*. The trend at the moment is to penalise the poorest of the poor by making them poorer. There is a world-wide call on rich nations to help poor nations. A Socialist Government such as ours should within its limited means begin implementing this call at the national level wherever possible.

Chapter IV

POLITICAL POWER AND CONTROL

Know the Party

What is UNIP? What must those of us who are in control make it to mean to the Common Man? The aims and objectives of the Party appear in Chapter I. These are in two sections showing what they were before and what they are after Independence. In both, it is obvious that service to Man is of paramount importance, that is, *Man is central in all that we think, say and do*.

The Party was not only designed to bring about independence, but also to maintain it. We must continue to make the Party a source and channel of the people's political thought and action, for only by the Party making itself a truly and genuine people's organisation and servant is it going to succeed in maintaining the same at Government level. It is common sense to say that Government institutions are even more complicated than those of the Party for they are many more and varied. Now we cannot succeed in making the Party a truly people's organisation unless we have understood precisely what its structure is, the checks and balances within it, and how it operates.

How UNIP is organised

Let us now begin with the structure of the Party. First, the United National Independence Party really started as a mass movement. It was successor to the Zambia African National Congress which broke away from the African National Congress to spearhead the people's independence movement in Northern Rhodesia. Right from the word go, it was clear that we set out to create a people's movement that would not only be the basis of fighting for and achieving independence but one that would stand the test of time to spearhead the people's development in all its aspects.

This firm base still stands today, and it is our intention to streamline this people's Party in such a way that it will continue to defend effectively our hard-won Independence, and at the same time fulfil the second objective of spearheading the development of the people.

The most important unit in the Party is the active single member in his community of families at the village level in rural areas or at the section level in urban areas. From here you have branches which consist of a number of villages in rural areas and a number of sections in towns. The constituency which comprises a number of branches is the next level of the Party's pyramid-like family tree. This leads on to the regional level from where we reach Freedom House, that is the Headquarters of the people's Party in the capital city.

Leadership at village and section levels is elected; so it is at branch and constituency levels, thereby providing a solid base for a democratic socialist state. At the regional level it can be elected or appointed by the Central Committee of the Party. The Central Committee is the Party's executive as well as administering body. It consists of fifteen members—eleven of them elected by the people at three-year intervals at an annual conference, and four nominated by the Party's President.

Regional officials are charged with the heavy responsibility of seeing that all Party affairs, organisational and otherwise, are carried out effectively in these regions. They also act as an effective two-way channel between the people, through their sections, village, branch and constituency organisations and the Party Headquarters on to Government.

Headquarters of the Party

Up to now the Party Headquarters has had only a full-time Administrative Secretary. The experience of the last three years shows clearly that Zambia's enemies are legion. To fight and defeat these we cannot find a better way than the Party being effectively organised.

Now, who are these enemies? First, within the Party. Human nature being what it is, we have got to think of those who might be apathetic, those who want to deviate from the Party line, either because they do not like discipline or simply because of their own selfish reasons. There is, of course, tribalism, provincialism, racialism and bureauracy. Of course, all these evils are dangers not only within the Party but perhaps even more so in Government.

Secondly, we have reactionary forces working twenty-four hours a day to try and cause confusion within Zambia by using all sorts of methods. These will be forces first from minority Governments whose philosophy is based on fear, whose Governments do not stem from all the people for fear of majority rule. Their aim, therefore, is to destroy UNIP and its leadership so that chaos could follow and then they can claim Zambia to be another Bantustan. As if this were not sufficient, you have the East and West power struggle right in our midst. Both the East and the West are struggling to influence the Party, the youth, labour movements, students, organisations, etc. They are not giving us time to reorganise our society. They realise only too well that if we become entrenched with the massive support that the Party enjoys today, in another couple of years it will be impossible to shake Zambia.

Through aid to us they send to Zambia some of their best men in the field of destroying Parties and Governments alike. All this calls for vigilance on our part. It means rising above the bigotry of tribalism, provincialism, racialism and bureaucracy.

The Party must give itself a new rôle in the field of political, economic, social and cultural development. This new rôle cannot be effectively implemented if we do not have an effective and full-time Secretary General under the Central Committee who will also be Minister without portfolio.

The rôle of the Party in the field of development

Here Ministers of State must reach the people through their Provincial Development Committees, whose membership will include at the political level all Political Assistants/Co-operatives and other Political Assistants, all Regional Secretaries, Rural Council Chairmen and on the Civil Service level will include all Provincial and District heads of Government departments. In their turn district leaders will have to work hard to see that they reach every corner of their district. The Regional Secretary shall be Chairman and the District Secretary, Secretary.

Again at this level all other agencies for development, apart from Civil Service heads of Government departments, shall be invited. Indeed, each District Councillor shall take charge of his ward in terms of development. Under the chairmanship of each Councillor that ward shall see to it that they plan for development in their ward with emphasis being laid on agricultural productivity. Emphasis shall be laid on villages forming productivity councils which might be the basis of future co-operative development.

Within this framework the villagers and peasants shall be encouraged to do the following, among other things:

(a) To use compost manure or fertilisers even if they are just using their ordinary hoes.

(b) To use oxen and hand ploughs.

(c) Cleanliness, thereby having healthy bodies.

(d) To find a supply of clean water for every home.

(e) Child care and how to use local foodstuffs properly.

(f) Cultural activities shall be encouraged seriously.

(g) As in the past, political activities will continue vigorously at this level with at least a weekly meeting to discuss current affairs under the Chairmanship of the Ward Councillor. If villages are too distant apart then the area shall be subdivided into a fitting number of sub-wards which the Councillor shall visit every week or fortnightly.

As development must always start from the known to the unknown, it is important that when we speak of productivity in the field of agriculture, a carefully laid out plan is introduced. It is well known that Zambia has some of the best soils in the world. The highest recorded yields for maize, groundnuts and cotton per acre are 8,000 lb. or 40 bags; 2,000 lb. or 11 bags; and 3,000 lb. respectively.

It follows, therefore, that if good soils are identified and our people prepare them properly, our expected targets at the end of our Four-Year Development Plan in 1970 will be realised. The following order of what might help us to produce more should therefore be looked at carefully:

(a) Good preparation of the soil, if necessary by the ordinary hoe, but emphasis to be laid on the use of oxen and hand plough.

(b) Early planting, proper spacing and use of improved seed.

(c) Application of compost manure or the right type of fertiliser in right quantities.

(d) Weeding at the right time.

There is one other message and this is to the youth of the country. The future of this nation lies in the importance we attach to our land. It is clear to our future planners that at least 50 per cent of our youth are going to have to find their future on the land. This is a good thing and is as it should be. What is required is that this message must be instilled into the minds of all of them in schools and homes alike.

Speaking of the importance the nation, and especially the youth, should attach to the land, it must be remembered that this nation has decided to have at least one Young Farmers' Club at every school in the country. This is now part and parcel of our life. Ministers and all other leaders will have to see that they visit and encourage our Young Farmers' Clubs whenever they visit schools.

It is important, for example, that we should demonstrate to every student in Zambia that a good living can be earned from the land, and at boarding schools that the whole school can learn to help feed itself by the labour of its people on the land. Indeed, every branch should have a Young Farmers' Club and Constituency leaders should see that this is done.

To achieve all this the Party must go all out to see that this proposed order, with changes where necessary, is implemented. Nothing can come without long and arduous hours of work. It can never be overemphasised that as we make this big drive our people should always be made to realise and appreciate the importance of working together as a team for the good of all as well as remembering the importance of that cohesiveness in our society that makes a mutual aid society an admirable way of life.

There is another point that must be made before we leave the question of the agrarian revolution. The Ministers of Agriculture and Education with their respective officials will soon start looking at how we can get more agricultural training done in all our schools, in, say, the following manner:

> Primary schools, for example, could teach good preparation of soil by the use of elementary tools, early planting, spacing, weeding and the use of insecticides. Secondary schools might include in their training oxen cultivation, improved seed, and the proper use of fertiliser. At the University level, mechanisation could be taught. Indeed, subjects like irrigation could be for Post-Graduates.

We aim at building hospitals and clinics all over the country thereby providing medical attention for every citizen and resident of Zambia. Still in the field of health we have almost eradicated small-pox and in this the Party and Government worked jointly, for which the nation is most thankful. Education is spreading like a wild bush fire to every corner of Zambia—another very effective way of distributing the wealth of the nation. The tax system is no longer aggressive. Fertiliser is being distributed, very often subsidised by Government; loans are being given to those who are prepared to work hard. Enlightened legislation to improve the lot of the worker has been enacted; indeed, there are a hundred and one things being done to raise the standards of living by the Party and Government.

We are, without beating drums and hitting gongs, well on the way to the establishment of a humanist's state.

We must emphasise, however, that unless this development starts within the people themselves, we cannot succeed. Leaders and workers within the Party and the Government must go all out— all out—to kindle the interest of the common man in his own personal development and emphasising at the same time that it is to be personal development to the advantage of all, not just an individual. Development means changing certain attitudes of our people that stand between them and a fuller life without necessarily destroying the good that has been discussed already in this pamphlet.

Finally, three years is not a long time but even with the little wealth we found and what little we have acquired during our time, we can rightly claim to have started distributing it fairly. But we have a long way to go and there is no room for complacency.

Chapter V

PROGRAMME FOR CONSOLIDATION OF HUMANISM IN ZAMBIA

Part One: The rôle of the Party

(*a*) The Party must strive relentlessly to establish in Zambia a true socialist state, based on the principles outlined in the preceding chapters.

(*b*) The Party must transform Zambia to become progressively a country in which there is equality and respect for human dignity.

(*c*) The Party must be vigilant about development of capitalist tendencies in Zambia; progressively the Party should work towards the elimination of privileges and inequalities among citizens.

(*d*) The Party must encourage *Hard Work*, *Self-reliance* and *Co-operative Effort* which form the basis of the Zambian way of life.

(*e*) The Party must encourage the revival of Zambian arts and crafts, acceptable customs and the development of national culture without thereby entrenching either provincialism or tribalism.

(*f*) No person, whatever his race, religion or colour can become a member of the Party unless he is prepared to accept the principles of Zambian Humanism.

Part Two: The rôle of Party leaders

(*a*) All Party leaders, that is all members of the Central Committee, Ministers, Members of Parliament and all officials, must openly declare their support for the principles of Zambian Humanism.

(*b*) All Party leaders must work actively to promote the accepted principles of Zambian Humanism.

(*c*) All Party leaders must abandon any practices or privileges which conform to capitalistic principles and not to the declared principles of Zambian Humanism.

Part Three: Land

(*a*) Land must remain the property of the State.

(*b*) In future, no person will be allowed to own land in perpetuity or to possess an exclusive interest in the land in perpetuity.

(*c*) The State may rent land to various users on behalf of the people.

Part Four: Industrial and agricultural development

(*a*) The policy of the Party outlined in Chapter III in relation to Industrial and Agricultural Development in Zambia will continue.

(*b*) The Party will place greatest emphasis on co-operative effort, especially in respect of agricultural development, although members of co-operative societies formed to promote industrial projects should be increased progressively.

(*c*) The Party's policy of encouraging private enterprise, within the framework of accepted Government policy, will continue.

(*d*) The Party will devise targets for industrial and agricultural production in order to provide the much-needed national incentive and to encourage realistic planning.

(*e*) The Party accepts that a rapid and widespread improvement of living standards of Zambians depends upon *maximum* utilisation of land for agricultural purposes and *hard work.*

Part Five: Co-operation and development

(*a*) Success in establishing a true humanist state will depend on co-operation between the Party leaders and leaders of persons in all walks of life in Zambia.

(*b*) Therefore, there is a need to establish rapidly a college in Zambia where the principles of Zambian Humanism can be studied and understood by all persons concerned with the promotion of development.

(*c*) The Party should encourage the formation of Village Productivity Councils, wherever possible.

(*d*) In schools, students should be taught the importance of collective effort in the context of principles of Zambian Humanism.

(*e*) Wherever possible, school authorities must encourage schoolchildren to maintain school gardens.

3

ZAMBIA TOWARDS ECONOMIC INDEPENDENCE*

His Excellency Dr K D Kaunda
President of the Republic of Zambia

PART I INTRODUCTION

Comrade Vice-President, Mr. Speaker, comrade National Chairman, comrades National Councillors, Guests, Friends and Countrymen.

Today we continue on our never-ending journey of discussing about the importance of man and planning for his all-round development.

Several times before, I have declared in very clear terms that political independence without matching economic independence is meaningless. It is economic independence that brings in its wake social, cultural and scientific progress of man. No doubt political independence is the key, but only the key to the house we must build.

. . . Now, we in Zambia are becoming known for our fearlessness in exposing our weaknesses and difficulties in human relations, especially politically. The time has now come for us to analyse and expose our weaknesses and difficulties in the field of economic development. Of course, we will do more than just expose our weaknesses and difficulties.

This National Council, and I hope all others to come, must pay more attention to the country's economic development than has been the case hitherto. We have, I am afraid, tended to see politics first instead of seeing MAN first in everything that we do. We must always remember that we fought and won independence for the sake of MAN, not for the sake of politics.

---

*Speech at the National Council of the United National Independence Party at Mulungushi, 19th April, 1968.

. . . If we are going to implement Humanism successfully, then let us remember that we have got to plan to serve the interests of MAN. All our institutions must be geared to serve the interests of the common man. This is an important point and I will repeat it in another way. If we are true humanists then whatever institutions we create must be geared towards fulfilling our commitments to the common man. Basically this means providing adequate food, adequate clothing and adequate shelter for *all* our people in Zambia and *not* just a few of them.

How do we achieve this? To answer this question effectively let us take some time to analyse what Zambia is economically. If, however, we are to understand what goes on in Zambia economically and put it to good use in terms of the Zambian's participation in this very important field, let us begin by appreciating what the Zambian humanist's approach to property ownership is. . . . To a humanist there is nothing wrong in owning some property. What is important in this is: how is that property accumulated and used?

Work and profit motive

The accumulation of property immediately reminds one of 'there is nothing for nothing'. In other words, to accumulate something we must work. The word 'work' reminds us of the 'profit motive', which is inherent in every human society. The profit motive taken to excess leads us on to the road of capitalism. On the other hand, whatever man does consciously or unconsciously has a strong element of profit motive. This, however, it should be pointed out, could be 'profit motive' in the interest of society as a whole or 'profit motive' in the interest of an individual.

May I repeat what I have said before and this is that with the impact of the money economy, our mutual aid society can never be the same again. Let me hasten to point out that I am not lamenting change at all . . . We welcome change; what we do not welcome is the diminishing of man's importance.

Need for stimulating Zambian individual initiative in Economic life

To go back to our subject, I do not think it is right for us to stifle Zambian individual initiative unless, of course, we do want to

continue to allow foreign capitalists to exploit us as a nation, which
they are doing at the moment. The very fact that we have declared
ourselves in favour of a mixed economy is more than an indication
that there is a place for individual initiative and, let me add here,
that no matter what is proclaimed from roof-tops I know of no
country, whether it is in the Eastern or Western world, where the
economy is not in some measure a mixed one today.

Humanism abhors exploitation of man by man

We cannot declare ourselves in favour of private enterprise,
and forbid Zambians from participating in the private sector. It is
important to remember, however, that as humanists we cannot
allow Zambians to develop into capitalists at all and here is where
a serious problem arises. In the final analysis, all this boils down to
one major point. Our society through its institutions—its man-made
institutions—must fight with all it has at its disposal against the
exploitation of man by man in whatever field.

How can we strive to achieve a society such as the one we are
aiming to establish? One thing is clear. It will not be an easy job.
Of course, we all know that nothing good has ever come without
working hard for it. In other words, Zambia must be prepared to
map out her own course. Broadly speaking, she must be prepared
to learn from others, as already pointed out, but in the end she
must be bold enough to make her own experiments, devise her own
ways and decide in the end which one of these will help stabilise
her society by putting development facilities at the disposal of all
our people in both our rural and urban areas.

Some of the experiments we make may be costly but in the end
we shall have learnt through trial and error and, to a young country
like Zambia, fighting for a place in the international community,
no lesson is better than the one which comes from trial and error.

Combating exploitation

(a) Zambian participation in business

The next question we must ask ourselves is—how can we stop
the exploitation of one man by another? We must be very frank
and look squarely into the face of this whole problem. Today
our society is being exploited very badly indeed by some unscrupu-
lous men and women who are driven to the extreme right by the

'profit motive'. A good number of them bring very little capital into Zambia, but because of their know-how they are able to build something locally on borrowed Zambian money and then send out of the country excessive profits after a very short time. It is difficult to stop such exploitation without first of all involving Zambians themselves. We have been watching this for the last three years. We can watch no longer. The last time I addressed you I spoke in terms of some of you joining the economic field and, indeed, a few have already gone. More must follow.

Even as I do this I am conscious of the fact that some of those who may join private enterprise may tend to project more capitalist instincts than humanist ones. However, society and the State are strong enough to handle such tendencies because I can assure you that we will do nothing to create Zambian capitalism here. I will hope to develop this point later.

Comrades, let me now go back to the question of Zambian participation in the economy of our country. I mentioned earlier that we should face squarely the difficulties that we experience in Zambia in so far as full control of our economy is concerned. We do not want to lament about the colonial past as it is only too well known that we were neglected by successive British Governments, but it would certainly be a complete waste of time to discuss that here. Our task is now to identify those difficulties that make it hard for us to control our own economy and then plan to do something about it.

(b) Foreign participation in Zambian economy in accordance with policy of non-alignment.

This is something which only we Zambians must do and no other person can do it for us. We must think and plan our own way and only when it comes to implementing it must we then throw our doors wide open to international participation in accordance with our non-alignment policy. We have no inhibitions about this because no matter how advanced we become we will still be part of the international community and we will have to give and take as we live and let live. Speaking of getting help from outside reminds one of the importance of using as much as possible what we have at home as the basis of nation-building and on to it we graft whatever we are able to get from outside whether this is capital, know-how or labour. I will hope to develop this point towards the end of my speech.

Process of nation-building

Let us now look at our own deficiencies in the process of nation-building, for only after we have effectively analysed this shall we know where to go and who to go to for the necessary extras. Further, to identify them let us categorise these necessities. Now, apart from these elements which provide us with the dynamo that makes every society tick we all know that one of the most serious handicaps that stands between us and the control of our country's economy is lack of education and training in various fields. Major among these are science and technology, commercial and agricultural training. To overcome this need in the shortest possible time we will have to tackle these problems much more vigorously than we have been able to do up to now, for time is not with us.

There is yet another field in which we must work hard. And this is generating interest in our people so that they can look at the economic development of the country as the most important cornerstone of nation-building. One must add that once interest is so generated we have also to work hard to keep it there.

Let it be emphasised, however, that the more we interest our people in this particular field the more they will be exposed to dangers I have referred to already—those of becoming a money-centered society. Wealth, like knowledge or any other instrument of service to man we can think of, becomes an instrument of oppression and suppression if we do not handle it properly. Very often we discuss the problem of distributing wealth equally among our people. There are many reasons why this is important. Major among these, however, are that we want each one of our four million people to live a fuller life and, secondly, wealth that is concentrated in the hands of a few people is a danger to any society in that those in whose hands wealth was centred would become exploiters of their fellow men in more than one way and this is no good both for those whom they exploit as well as for themselves.

Any form of exploitation of one man by another is to be fought in Zambia; we hope not only by this generation but also by generations to come. Why do we feel so strongly about this? Before our political independence the combination of political and economic exploitation of so many racial groups by the dominant one made Zambia a very sad country to live in. In this particular field life is no longer so. The people's Parliament has continually been passing revolutionary measures to change this. We will continue to make these efforts as time goes on.

Humanism: need for hard work and self-reliance

Now, as I have said before, we must open the economic stream to Zambian participation. We have no choice but to swim in this stream so that we can learn by doing. For Zambians, that wealth, like knowledge or any other instrument of service to man, must be acquired before it can be used. In this respect I am emphasising two points: the need for self-reliance and hard work and the need for us to strike an equilibrium so that our society is not destroyed by the upsurge in our people of the instinct to accumulate more and more wealth so that in the end it is done at the expense of the importance of man.

We must be careful. The society we are determined to build is one in which, through every individual's maximum contribution to the national whole, we shall provide for each and every one of us, in the shortest possible time, a fuller life. What do we mean by a fuller life and how does this come about? Putting it briefly, this means everyone in society being provided with decent food, decent clothes and decent shelter. These will only come about through the combined efforts of the State on one hand and the maximum contribution of each and every individual in any given society to the general whole.

Economic reforms of the nation

So far I have discussed with you various aspects of Humanism mainly as it governs the relations between human beings and wealth in our man-centred Zambian society. I have indicated that I would soon be putting forward the policy of Humanism in action insofar as the march towards control of the economy by Zambians is concerned. This is the subject I intend to develop now. Let me emphasise that I intend to lay out the foundations for major economic reform of the nation to enable it to achieve its goal of economic independence under Humanism.

PART II AGRICULTURAL SECTOR

Comrades and Friends, if we intend to develop Zambia very quickly then we must work very hard at the means of involving all our people in these important economic, social, cultural, scientific and indeed political activities. Without their participation nothing will be achieved. The family tree on which we have got to base our activities to achieve this all-round development of the common man is what we have discussed before.

There is Man the individual; there is Man within the family headed by the head of that family; there is Man within the village headed by the village headman; there is Man within the ward headed by the Ward Councillor; there is Man within the District headed by the Regional Secretary and the District Secretary who are, respectively, Chairman and Secretary of the District Development Committee. Indeed, there is Man within the Province headed by the Minister of State with his Provincial Development Committee; finally, you have Man in the whole country with headquarters in Lusaka.

I want to see the implementation of the Plan shifted in theory and practice to Provincial and District Committees and I hope that we will be able to discuss this issue at this National Council. Countrymen and friends, allow me to discuss with you some general problems of planning in developing countries. Needless for me to say Zambia is one of them.

Balanced economic development

In the history of early modernisation and industrialisation—and in many developing countries today—rapid economic growth was and is the superior aim of the planners. But to reach this aim they were often only concerned with the question of high and higher investments at all cost and with the destination of priorities of industry over agriculture or vice versa. All other structural aspects of development were often simply neglected. The question of a balance between regions, between industries, between scales of production, between techniques, and between other economic and social aspects was given little attention.

There are many examples in the West as well as in the East, where in the heavy industrial sector which was given priority, the establishment of very big projects with the most sophisticated, 'latest' methods of production was a practice taken for granted, and was

not made a problem of choice between alternatives. So the consequence was that the possibilities for a suitable substitution of
labour for capital, that is the removal of unemployment, was not
seen and as a result a big part of rural manpower remained *underemployed* instead of being used for productive purposes.

Even today, when you look at some African, Asian and Latin-
American countries you will recognise that development and progress
is understood as development and progress in a European or
American way. The prevailing ideas, attitudes, techniques, etc.,
reflect too often the European and American 'way of life'. Especially
the imported means of production and consumer goods do neither
functionally nor materially rely on the conditions available in a
developing country.

Economic development: labour intensive techniques

For example, we all here know that one oxen plough replaces
already about eight labourers working with a hoe; one tractor,
properly utilised, replaces at least ten oxen ploughs or one hundred
and sixty people working with hoes! You can imagine what it would
mean and what would follow our employing tractors and other
highly sophisticated and highly capital-intensive equipment *everywhere* in the country.

If we equate development and progress only with the number of
tractors used, with the number of big projects, with a small number
of well looking areas, and with the town only, then we will soon
face very big problems: we will not be able to avoid greater unemployment at the end of a year and much more so, at the end of
our Four Year Development Plan. Development that is restricted to
only a small part of the economic sector, to only a few regions, to
only large-scale production, and to only highly capital-intensive
techniques is, in my view, no development at all.

These described and often prevailing facts in many countries
make it absolutely necessary to follow a different orientation of
economic planning. Economic planning must learn to see the virtues
of rural development, of small industrialisation; it must realise
the potential in utilising human beings where they are and in reaching
a self-sustained growth in all the regions and sectors of the economy.

That means that the unutilised potential lying in the unemployed
or *underemployed human capital* must be fully grasped and adequate

measures and planning methods found to deal with the problem. True development must be orientated to involve people into the development process as much as possible. Let me now come down to earth and discuss Zambia's problems instead of generalising. Zambia's economy, as we all know, is a mixed one, that is, the State, co-operatives and private firms work side by side. We have acknowledged in the past, we do so now, the importance of private capital's participation. It must be emphasised, however, that this coexistence must be a co-ordinated and confident one. It does the country and the economy no good if these agents work against one another as I will point out later.

Simultaneous development of agriculture and industry

There is another point I would like to bring out and this is that it is important that we put in motion a simultaneous development of all sectors of the economy to avoid a one-sided structure, for only in this way can we successfully mobilise the initiative of both the industrial worker and that of the peasant. We must do away with the outmoded approach of looking at the various aspects of our economic development through divisive spectacles of industry versus agriculture or of heavy industry versus light industry, etc.

Rural development: a priority

The third point I want to mention is regional development. Up to now regional development has been the privilege of the line-of-rail provinces. This we can no longer accept for now we have a People's Government. The basis for the creation of a genuine and balanced regional development is the decision to spread economic activity and to give considerably more weight to the development of the underdeveloped areas within the country.

Today there is so much talk, but very little action, of developed countries helping developing ones. We must fight this within our own country. I hope when I come to deal with the commercial and industrial sectors I will show how we might do this.

Regional development planning

However, in so far as we are concerned, the decision has been taken. Humanism in Zambia is a decision in favour of rural areas. It must now be the task of our planning and research authorities in Lusaka, in the provincial headquarters and the district ones, to formulate regional plans, to determine basic data of a series of factors and the boundaries of viable economic areas. Once so equipped they should determine a system of regionally developing centres which are large enough to maintain the economic and social establishments and activities that are well suited for industrial development. Apart from this, and this is very important, special promotional and organisational measures for the development of small-scale industries in rural areas must be taken.

Having dealt with the overall framework of our development, I now want to address myself to some specific points of agricultural policy.

Training programmes and rural extension policy

The unsatisfactory stage of development in our Agriculture is by no means the sole fault of our farmers. The established system takes a good share of the blame. Our people in the villages are prepared to work hard if they see a chance that they can benefit from their effort (they had to do so in the past merely to survive). It is our responsibility to provide them with the means and I am convinced that they will grasp these opportunities to improve themselves. We will have to reorganise our training programmes and our rural extension policy. Our women, who have been completely neglected in the past, must be included in this new strive in training and extension.

Assistance to small farmers

We must provide for the people in the villages the know-how through education, with the means to produce more by supplying them with good seeds, fertiliser and equipment they can handle. At the present stage we don't have to teach complicated methods of handling sophisticated machinery which very often are more of a liability than an asset to our village farmers. Many of the essential methods of modern farming are quite simple things. For example, use of good seeds, use of fertiliser, proper planting, etc. At the present stage there is no need for us to go for costly mechanisation in our farming industry. First of all we must use our available resources to the full extent, and then, and only then, should we think of using labour-saving equipment.

Agricultural development: need to use available resources

We have millions of people living in the rural areas. Give them a chance first to earn a little more than the present subsistence. We have hundreds of thousands of oxen in our villages, which don't cost us money. Let us use them first before we spend millions of Kwacha on more and more tractors. Let us use those things first that we already have before we start crying for more.

The Government is also responsible for providing the required structures to encourage development in our farming sector throughout the country. The whole land tenure system must be geared to provide those securities needed to encourage investments to improve the land, required by a modern agriculture. But we must avoid a rigid system, often accompanied by private ownership of the land. I have stated over and over again that the basis of our rural development must start at village level with the approximate 450,000 small family farms in existence. We must provide these thousands of farm units with the means to become an integrated part of our cash economy. It is not our intention to use public funds to create huge, heavily mechanised production units of any sort where a few selected individuals act as shareholders on Government enterprises who, without contributing much in effort, make a good living. If an individual, through hard work and devotion, builds up his small unit to a viable commercial farm, we will be happy to see him emerge, but we will not spend public money to create a few agricultural capitalists. We need commercial farms; we are lucky to have efficient commercial farms, they serve an important purpose in our farming system, but these must rest on the hard work and devotion of the farmers themselves.

The Government is willing to provide them with the services they require and which they cannot provide themselves. Our main emphasis must rest with those thousands of farm units which we must help to emerge from strict subsistence level into a living relationship with the rest of our cash economy. If we look at our present production system and the demand on agricultural products we will see the need to set priorities of agricultural expansion. The most immediate needs to expand production are the fields of livestock products, oil seeds, rice, fruits and vegetables and cotton.

Agricultural expansion: priorities

(a) Livestock

The demand for meat is rapidly increasing. At present we have just a vague idea of the real demand for meat in the country. Our problem of malnutrition is directly connected with our insufficient supply of animal protein. To solve this problem we have to improve the supply of meat and make it available to all our people. In 1964 the internal production of meat and meat products supplied 65 per cent of the demand, this year we will only be able to supply about 35 per cent of the demand. To change this rather gloomy picture it will be necessary to look for a completely new approach to the problem. On the beef market we are in a rather difficult position. The natural conditions for beef production are fairly good and the size of our national herd would, under similar conditions in other parts of the world, be sufficient to supply the country with all the beef required. In 1964–65 we were able to produce 67,400 head of cattle for slaughtering, whereas in 1966–67 only 50,965 head were brought to the markets. It must be the task of this Government to encourage our village farmers to improve the management standard of their herds and to look at the cattle as a ready source of cash. It is a social and political problem we face here which we can only solve through education. Merely shouting at our village farmers will not help. But there are other sources of meat supply. During the last few months I have been emphasising the extension of our underdeveloped pig industry. In many parts of the world pigs are the main supplier of meat. For us this might be a new thing, but we must think up new ideas to solve our problems.

(b) Pigs

Pig production could well be, especially in those areas with maize surplus, an additional source of income to our farmers. On the Continent of Europe, for example, a thriving meat industry developed around pig production, establishing a valuable agro-industry and supplying the population with animal protein required for their health. We should not deny ourselves these possibilities because it is a new thing but we must look carefully into this aspect so that we are able to solve our problems.

(c) Eggs and milk

Before I move on to another field let me refer you, Countrymen, to an important declaration I made on Independence Day. I am here referring to an egg and a pint of milk a day for every Zambian by December, 1970. In so far as egg production is concerned, I will say something about it later. For now let me discuss with you the problem of milk production. I have just been dealing with the importance of changing our attitudes in so far as pig production is concerned. We in Zambia are used to cow milk; I fear that we will not reach our target by December 1970 if we do not think of other methods of getting milk. I am made to understand that in some countries abroad goat milk is used very extensively. I am, therefore, appealing to the country as a whole through the Ministries of Agriculture, Co-operatives, Youth and Social Development and Presidential Affairs, that is, the Provincial and District Government wing of it, and indeed through the Party, to study this whole issue. It should be fairly easy for every village in the country, with a few exceptions of course, to rear goats. If a certain type of goat produces more milk, then, for goodness sake, let us import it in good numbers after the necessary research and experiment have been done. Further, I understand that goat milk is very rich and I see no reason why we should not try this.

(d) Groundnuts

Another important task we face is the expansion of our groundnut production. In 1966 we had to import vegetable oil or oil seeds to the tune of K2 million, despite the fact that in most parts of our country groundnuts grow very well. For a large part of the groundnut production in the Eastern Province we have a valuable market for high quality confectionery nuts which we are not utilising to the full extent. I see no reason why this country should not be able to double the groundnut production within two years providing us with the vegetable oil we need and valuable protein for human and animal consumption. It is a challenge which concerns all of us, the farmer in the village, the civil servant and the political leader. Groundnut production is suitable for the smallest farm unit and we cannot allow ourselves to fail here.

(e) Cotton

Our cotton production is well under way but we have to expand the production tremendously to meet the demand of our emerging textile industry. By 1970 we will require 3,000 tons of lint to feed this industry and by that time we must produce that in the country. Cotton is a crop well suited for the remoter, dryer areas of the country. The yields achieved, for example, in the Luangwa Valley, the Eastern Province Plateau, the Southern Province, especially the Gwembe Valley, are first-class and I urge the farmers to give priority to this crop instead of maize. The Extension Service in the Ministry of Agriculture as well as political and other leaders must do all in their power to promote cotton growing in areas where there are no economic outlets for other crops. Cotton is a crop suitable for our small-scale family farms and might provide them with a good return if they look after the crop properly.

(f) Rice

In 1966 we had to import all our demands of rice valued at K440,000 (40,000 bags). The climate in the country is suitable to produce this crop and we have areas in this country where rice will grow well. Yet we are not producing any significant quantity of this important commodity and indeed in future there might be more economic export markets for rice than we might even hope to find for our maize surplus. I am glad that the Ministry responsible is carrying out surveys and experiments to try and develop the techniques required for large-scale production in our country.

(g) Vegetables

Again, in 1966 we had to spend K1.1 million to import vegetables in various forms. In some of our rural areas we produce vegetables but the producers cannot find a market for their products. Yet we import canned beans and peas from Europe, sweet corn from California, etc. Nearly all these imported vegetables grow in Zambia yet we are not able to produce and process them here. Some of our experts say the market for these products is too small or that we cannot produce enough vegetables to warrant the establishment of a canning factory in our rural areas. This is wrong. We cannot expect our farmers to produce before they have a market for their vegetables. We must be prepared to provide the canning factory to encourage production on a scale to warrant that investment.

(h) Fruit

Citrus, bananas, avocados and other tropical fruits grow well in nearly all parts of the country. In the Eastern Province near Katete

I have seen oranges which could compete with the high quality fruits imported from outside. Citrus concentrates we have to import from various countries which we could produce ourselves. I find in many of our villages throughout our country a good number of fruit trees, yet because of lack of water and, I think, know-how, the people are not able to look after their trees properly at all. Yet we all know that vitamins are essential for the good health of our people, especially that of our children. Some people argue that a citrus tree needs seven years before it starts to produce fruits. But if we don't start to plant the trees now, we never will be able to harvest the fruits. I want a fruit industry established to supply the needs of our urban population; I want to see fruit trees planted in the villages to supply the local needs. At present it is nearly impossible for an individual in Lusaka to obtain a citrus tree for his garden, not to speak of the impossibility for a villager to obtain such trees. We must ensure we make fruit trees and seeds available for our people, otherwise the situation will remain as it is.

(i) Poultry

Since 1964 we have been able to increase our poultry production by 140 per cent but, of course, we are still a long way off from self-sufficiency. There are still millions of Zambians who are not able to get a bird on their table at least once a week. We are very far away from making it possible for every Zambian to have an egg once every day. Now, as I have pointed out already, we have done extremely well in this particular field but, I repeat, much more remains to be done. I have already sent to Ministers of State for Provinces, who are Chairmen of our Provincial Development Committees, a paper which I hope we have all seen and which paper we must discuss before the end of this National Council. In this, as you all know by now, is contained the plan for organising our Women's Co-operative Movement on a revolutionary basis.

Need to involve women and youth in agrarian revolution

A word on our women's participation in our Agrarian Revolution. Those of us in this country who recall the times of our struggle for our political independence will remember that the attainment of independence might have been delayed without the very active part played by our mothers. If today we want to attain our Agrarian

Revolution in record time we must involve our mothers in this field very, very actively indeed. I am glad to say that wherever I have been in the country I have found wonderful response to the call I have made to them; and all I say is, all of us organisers, whether we are politicians or civil servants, must now go flat out to involve our mothers in this very, very important sector of the Zambian economy. I keep reminding you, Countrymen, that for the next 50 years or so the majority of our people will simply have to live on the land. We must, therefore, avoid making the errors which other countries, old and young, have made by neglecting their agricultural sector of the economy. I cannot overemphasise the importance of youth participation in this revolution. Every struggle that is not spearheaded or supported by the youth will not succeed. For one thing, like mothers they are fearless; secondly the future of the country depends very much on how we shape the young ones of today. It is our responsibility, therefore, to show them the way and prepare them to shoulder their responsibilities. I want to repeat this message to all our youth in the country today. Most of you are growing up not knowing what the fight for independence meant, for reading about it in books is not the same thing as participating in it. A few of you are misled and become scornful of your elders because you have more chances, which have been provided, by the way, for you because of the blood which flowed, because of the sacrifices which these noble sons and daughters of Zambia made so that you should be able to live a fuller life. You will not become leaders simply because you belong to the youth of today. This nation will choose its leaders from among those who are responsible, those who realise, understand and appreciate the importance of man and his position in all things on earth.

To be a leader at any level at all and in any scheme of things you have got to love your fellow human beings, you have got to be ready to sacrifice for their good, you have got to be able to learn to respect the feelings of your fellow men. Even as I say all this I am conscious of the fact that the task of preparing the young people of today is a responsibility that must be shared between them and us. We must provide the facilities in the firm belief that the youth will respond and fit in the scheme of things.

To come back to the subject of the Agrarian Revolution this is so important that I cannot end my remarks on the agricultural sector of our economy without referring to the part youth clubs in schools, as well as outside, will play to make this a success. I have already pointed out that when those of us who are Members of Parliament tour various regions from time to time we will be required to record certain development activities and in this record a place for the youth is assured.

Markets for agricultural products

Having discussed so much in so far as the promotion of the agricultural sector of our economy is concerned, I would like to remind the Council of the resolution they passed in the Matero Hall in October 1966 on the important subject of markets for our agricultural products. I have already pointed out, for example, that to expect our people to grow plenty of vegetables before we find them markets is a negative approach to the development of agriculture in Zambia. I am glad to report progress here, and this is that we are just about to complete the process of centralising our market facilities. As soon as this is over, and we hope it will be some time this year, we will make known how we will in practice tackle this very important subject.

PART III COMMERCIAL AND INDUSTRIAL SECTOR

Having dealt with the agricultural sector, I will now move on to the commercial and industrial economic activity. Economic activity in this field is dominated by four types of enterprise. These are—

1. State Enterprise;
2. Zambian Private Enterprise;
3. Foreign Controlled Enterprise; and
4. Resident Expatriate Enterprise.

First I want to talk about the last mentioned—The Resident Expatriate Enterprise. Economic activity in Zambia is dominated by European and Asian business communities whose members have been residents of this country for many years. Since Independence my Ministers and I have been making repeated appeals to the members of these communities, calling on them to identify themselves with the nation and urging them to Zambianise their businesses as soon as possible. I am very pleased to say that many have responded to our pleas, and have identified themselves with the country by taking up Zambian nationality and by making sincere efforts to train Zambians to skilled and executive positions. There is, however, an appreciably large number of others who have chosen to remain outside the national family. They have kept only one foot in Zambia in order to take advantage of the economic boom created by the Transitional and the First National Development Plans. The other foot they have kept outside Zambia in South Africa, Britain, Europe, India, or wherever they come from, ready to jump when they have made enough money, or when they think that the country no longer suits them. I am afraid the period of grace is over. These people must now make a final choice. We do not wish to keep them here against their will. We are a proud nation. At the same time it is not fair that we should allow them to make off with the jam and the butter and leave crumbs of dry bread for our people.

Need for economy to be in Zambian businessmen's hands

Comrades, time is now that we must take urgent and vigorous steps to put Zambian business firmly in the hands of the people themselves just as political power is in their hands. This must be done because experience shows that since Independence we have tried to assist the Zambian public with loans as well as know-how in the firm hope that in this way we would establish and build up Zambian entrepreneurship. I regret to report to the nation that this method has been very slow and, I am afraid, it has failed. We can lend very little money to our people and this is mainly for fixed capital development. If they run short of working capital they are unable to obtain credit facilities to see them through. The banks, the insurance companies, the building societies, the hire purchase companies and the other commercial financial institutions have not been very willing to assist the Zambian businessman. So the level of Zambian business has remained low and unless we take firm action now our Zambian businessmen will never catch up with the level of the resident expatriate businessman. These people have access to loan funds from banks, building societies, insurance companies, hire purchase companies, and every financial institution that exists in the country. It is therefore time to take more drastic steps to assist the People's business to bridge the gap that exists between it and the resident expatriate business.

Limiting local borrowing by resident expatriate enterprise

As the number one measure, I intend to direct my Minister of Finance to pass an instruction that the local borrowings of expatriate enterprise are to be controlled in the same way as the borrowings of foreign controlled enterprises are controlled. What I mean is this: from now on the banks, the building societies, the insurance companies, the hire purchase companies and all the other financial institutions in the country, before approving a loan for business purposes to a company or partnership or an individual businessman, must ascertain that—

    (a) If it is a company its members, its shareholders are Zambians, that is they have Zambian passports or green national registration cards.

    (b) If it is a partnership, that all the partners are Zambian, they have Zambian passports or green national registration cards.

    (c) If it is an individual, that he is a Zambian with a Zambian passport or green national registration card.

If the application for a loan or for an overdraft comes from a person who is not a Zambian citizen, then it must be referred to the Exchange Control authorities who will approve it or reject it using the same criteria as they use now in order to approve or reject applications for loans from foreign-controlled companies.

As you know, in this country we do not allow foreign companies to come and borrow money here without limits. The money they can borrow locally depends on the amount they bring into the country. The same type of criteria will therefore be applied to the resident expatriate businesses. Whether they are allowed to obtain loans locally will depend on the amount of their own investment and the type of business which they operate. Of course, all the resident expatriate businesses which operate here at the moment, whether companies, partnerships or individually owned businesses, already enjoy substantial loan and overdraft facilities. I do not want to force them to repay these loans immediately. If I did, I would be pushing them into financial troubles and I want to be fair. I do not therefore intend to call up their loans and overdrafts immediately. The Minister of Finance will give them a period of grace to repay these loans and reduce their overdrafts according to the size of the business and the rate they can afford to pay every month.

Credit facilities for Zambian businessmen

Now having done that I hope that the banks, the building societies and the other financial institutions will utilise their excess liquidity to assist Zambian business. I know that so far they have concentrated in helping the people they know and with whom they have dealt for many years. But they must realise that they operate in a free Zambia with Zambian money and they must get to know the Zambian people and the Zambian businessmen in order to be able to assess their ability and credit-worthiness, in the same way as they have learnt to assess expatriate businessmen. After all, let me remind the banks, the bulding societies, the insurance companies, the hire purchase companies and the other financial institutions once again; they operate in Zambia and they are using Zambian people's money.

Limiting resident expatriate business to certain areas

The second action I propose to take to help the Zambian enter-prise to develop is to give it certain areas in which to operate without competition from expatriate businesses. By areas I mean geographical areas and business areas. Looking back on the methods of the colonial regime of the past I notice that most of the Zambian businesses have developed in the townships where competition from expatriate business was not allowed. I do not know precisely why they did this. My guess would be that since the colonialists were preoccupied with the creation of artificial classes in order to 'divide and rule' they were in this form of discrimination trying to create a new class which they could use as a buffer when it came to dealing with the masses of our people who were already politically conscious. To go back to the point, however, they did not grant trading licences to expatriates in those areas and in this way a small group of Zambian business was established there. For reasons which are more human I intend to use their method and confine the areas of retail trading by resident expatriate businesses to the centres of the big towns only. By centres I mean what used to be called in the old days first-class trading areas, and I shall leave it to the legislators to fix the details. As far as I am concerned trading and bar licences from now on must only be granted or renewed in all other areas of the country if the applications come from a company or co-operative whose members or shareholders are Zambians, a partnership whose partners are all Zambians or an individual who is a Zambian. And by Zambian I repeat that I mean a Zambian citizen, a man with a Zambian passport or green national registration card. If the application comes from anybody else it must not be granted or the licence must not be renewed.

Future business trends in centres of large towns and cities

Now I am going to talk about the so-called first-class trading areas. It pains me to see that three and a half years after Independence there is not a single Zambian-owned business in Cairo Road. There is not even a resident expatriate business or a foreign controlled business or any business for that matter with a Zambian manager in Cairo Road. If there is one I shall be very pleased to hear about it, but it must be a very small business or I would certainly have come across it already. The same applies to the centre of Kitwe, Ndola, Chingola and all the large towns in the country. Obviously we cannot go on like this and in order to accelerate the change I shall direct that no additional trading licences will be granted in these areas except to Zambian companies, Zambian partnerships and Zambian individuals. So no new trading licences will be granted to a resident expatriate enterprise or to foreign companies in these areas. This, I think, takes care of the retail trading reforms. Before I finish on the subject I want to mention the towns where resident expatriate businesses will be allowed to operate. They are Chingola, Mufulira, Kitwe, Luanshya, Ndola, Kabwe, Lusaka, Mazabuka, Choma and Livingstone. These are the only places where resident expatriate retail businesses can continue to operate. Everywhere else I am giving them sufficient notice that their trading licences will not be renewed. They can find Zambians to sell their shops to. Alternatively, of course, and this I would also welcome, they can apply to become Zambians themselves.

Establishment of small markets in towns

In addition to this, however, I want to create more small-size trading places right through the country. For some time now I have been thinking about our system of having one large market in each town, sometimes two or three if the town is big and I do not think that this is satisfactory. I want small markets in each town instead. In other words, instead of a small number of large markets I want a large number of small markets. This will have many positive advantages. First it will provide better service to the community, for when there are many small markets in a town they can be placed conveniently to serve the various housing areas in each town and in this way our people would not have to walk long distances in order to do their shopping. The second advantage of importance is that we will be able to look after our small markets better than we can ever hope to do with the present big ones. In other words, it will be easier for us to keep them clean and so they will be more hygienic. A third important reason is that the more markets we have the more the number of market vendors we will have and so these small markets will provide us with additional employment opportunities.

Establishment of restaurants, tea-rooms and cafès in towns and cities

I hope that the Mayors, the City Councillors, the Municipal Councillors, and the members of Local Councils who are present here have taken note of what I have said. I want a large number of small markets in every city and town in the country, and I want every City Council, every Municipal Council, every Local Council to start making arrangements to build them. This reminds me of something else that our towns lack. This is eating places: restaurants, tea-rooms, cafes, etc. All the people who work in the centre of towns and have to spend their lunch hour there because their homes are too far away, have to make do with a bun and a mineral for lunch which they buy from street vendors. Travellers from one town to another sometimes have to go without meals altogether until they reach their destination because there are no eating places on the way. This is not satisfactory. Apart from the hardship that this is causing our people, it is affecting the productivity of the Nation. A bun and a mineral may fill you up but it does not nourish you. I would therefore like to see thousands of these eating places, big and small, clean and tidy, built throughout the country—where our people will be happy to buy eggs, milk, fish, meat and vegetable foods, fresh fruit juices (from citrus and other fruits) and indeed places where I would like to see more use made of our other local foodstuffs as recommended by the Food and Nutrition Commission.

Granting of road services licences

The next field where I see no reason why Zambian enterprise should not operate as successfully as expatriate enterprise is transport. I will be directing the Minister of Transport not to grant any road services licences for buses, for lorries, for vans, for taxis, for any type of vehicle except to companies or co-operatives who have at least 75 per cent of their members or shareholders Zambians, to partnerships whose partners are Zambians or to Zambian individuals. All the resident expatriate transport organisations operating in these fields now will continue only to the expiry of their present road services licences. When these expire they can sell their businesses to Zambian co-operatives because their licences are not going to be renewed.

Granting of building material permits

The third field I would like to invite Zambian co-operatives to exploit is the contracting field, which involves the digging and transportation of sand, soil, clay, stone, etc. There is a licence in this country called a Building Mineral Permit which people who wish to extract sand or any of the other building minerals must obtain. From now on I direct my Minister of Lands and Mines not to give a building mineral permit to anybody except to a co-operative or company whose members or shareholders are Zambians, to a partnership whose partners are Zambians or to Zambian individuals—it should be emphasised that preference will be given to co-operatives, public companies and other group approaches over individual approaches. In this way, from now on I foresee that all business for the excavation and transportation of sand, soil and stone; all quarries, brick-fields and so on, will be owned and operated by Zambians. All expatriates who have such enterprises will run them until the end of their present permits. After that they will have to sell them to Zambians if they have not by then become Zambians themselves.

Sub-contractors to large companies should be Zambians

There are many other opportunities in the contracting field where Zambians can be successful. I understand that large companies, including the mining companies, quite often employ sub-contractors to do small jobs for them, such as digging trenches, clearing roads, painting houses, etc. These sub-contractors so far have often been expatriates. But these jobs can be done just as well, if not better, by Zambians. There are many people on the Copperbelt who have worked for many years on the Mines, and they have been in charge of labour gangs. I am sure that they can perform just as efficiently as some of the expatriate small contractors do. I do not intend to take any administrative action at this stage. All I want to do is to tell the Mining Companies that they must now look into the question of how they are to Zambianise their sub-contractors. I also intend to ask the Chairman of the Zambianisation Committee to look into this matter and report progress to me. If this approach is not listened to by the big companies, we will have to take other steps to implement it.

Awarding of PWD contracts of less than K100,000 to Zambian businessmen

A way in which the Government itself will assist Zambian contractors is that from now on the Public Works Department will award contracts worth less than K100,000 only to Zambians. The only people allowed to compete for these jobs will be co-operatives or companies all of whose members or shareholders are Zambians; and partnerships of Zambians, or individual Zambian builders. Again I must stress that Zambians are Zambian citizens, people with Zambian passports and green registration cards, and nothing else will be taken into account in deciding whether or not a man is a Zambian. I have talked about restricting resident expatriate businesses by making it more difficult for them to borrow money, and by keeping them out of certain geographical areas and certain types of business. All these measures are going to create very favourable conditions for the People's business to develop.

Need for Zambain enterprise to develop in accordance with the philosophy of Humanism

Humanism recognises the importance of private initiative in the economic development of the Nation. But at the same time, it abhors the exploitation of human beings by other human beings. I shall be watching the development of Zambian enterprise, and at the same time I shall be watching its behaviour—co-operatives, companies, partnerships or individuals alike. If it takes any unfair advantage of the privileged position in which we are putting it; if I see that the prices in Zambian retail shops are higher than those in the expatriate shops; if I hear that Zambian workers are not paid proper wages, if they are not provided with housing; if the contributions to the National Provident Fund and Workmen's Compensation Board are not paid regularly; if I hear that the Zambian businessmen are in any way dishonest with our Tax Department, then the Zambian businessmen will be dealt with very firmly indeed whether they are co-operatives, companies, partnerships, or individuals. I want them to develop so that they can be of service to their fellow human beings. In other words, I do not want them to get rich at the expense of the rest of the nation. Exploitation, whether it is done by people of one racial group against another or done by people of the same racial group against their own kith and kin, is wrong and we will not glorify it here in Zambia by allowing it a place. We are fiercely determined to fight it wherever it shows its ugly head. Even as I say this, Comrades, I know that this is not an easy thing to fight. Let me emphasise that I want Zambian businesses to expand and to prosper. But, for goodness sake, I do not propose to create Zambian capitalism here. This is incompatible with my conception of Humanism. I want to see the co-operative spirit develop. I want to see the businesses operating as co-operatives or as companies rather than as individuals. If they operate as companies I want to see that when they have achieved success they will give the opportunity to their fellow Zambians to share their profits.

Zambia Stock Exchange: its place in economic development

For this reason I intend to direct the Minister of Finance to set up a Stock Exchange here, so that the companies can become public companies instead of private ones (that is, they will have many members instead of just two or three), and make their shares available to the public. I want to see all the people of Zambia, whatever their occupation, participate in the economic development of the nation and at the same time get the opportunity to make higher earnings from their savings than the interest they can now earn on their savings accounts. Without meaning to sound apologetic for the capitalist system of a Stock Exchange, it is important to point out that it is very much better to have an investment made in a co-operative or a public company than have that money spent on beer or other intoxicating liquors. After all, any excessive profits made by that company will be taxed. This Stock Exchange approach, therefore, is the lesser of the two evils and the National Council must welcome this. When the time comes, I shall see that responsible Ministers set the limits of the Zambian enterprise that can remain a purely private enterprise. These limits will be based on the amount of capital employed, on turnover and on the number of employees. When an enterprise grows beyond these limits, then it must become a public company. When it grows even further, it will be taken over by the State. This is another warning I must make straight away. We do not propose to make of Zambians business barons now or in future. Everybody's contribution must ultimately be for the benefit of MAN through the State.

State enterprise

I am not saying this in order to discourage people. On the contrary, I shall be the first to congratulate and admire a businessman who has managed to create a very large enterprise. It shows initiative and ability. But, at the same time, I want them to see my point of view that when they get very big then they must come and work for the State, for the benefit of Zambia as a whole. *I do not want to create capitalism here.* Now is the time to give you my plans as regards State Enterprise. So far we have tried to promote State Enterprise the hard way. We have confined our new business activities through the Industrial Development Corporation to certain special types of enterprise, which have generally been the hardest type to develop. Some have been where the Government had to have control because such businesses were a strategic necessity. This happened in the case of the oil pipeline. Sometimes we invested in businesses where the risks were too great for private capital, or too much capital was needed and private enterprise was unable or unwilling to provide it, or the returns appeared too low for private enterprise, but the project was nevertheless necessary in the national interest. We also engaged in business where we wanted to influence prices and profitability. Examples are the Zambian National Wholesale Corporation Ltd., and the Zambia Steel and Building Supplies Limited.

Major faults of resident expatriate business

All along we were painfully aware that while we were entering into all the most difficult fields, resident expatriate business was taking advantage of the economic boom and making excessive profits. We tried to admonish them, even pleaded with them, but the major faults of these businesses are still not corrected. They operate price rings with similar companies and create a false monopoly position because of buoyant demand and the difficult supply position. They do not make enough efforts to move away from unacceptable sources of supply and outdated management philosophies. They still maintain personnel and training policies which are not in accord with the Nation's present needs. They are failing to reinvest a sufficient portion of their profits for general expansion and development. Obviously we cannot remain passive observers to these practices. We have to safeguard the national economy and prevent unfair exploitation of the present boom conditions. The field that has suffered most so far is the construction industry. Because of the pressure of demand and difficult supply position, prices have soared to astronomic heights. We have looked into the matter very carefully and have come to the conclusion that the reason for high building costs is not always the contractor's excessive profiteering. There are enough contractors in the country and we keep bringing new ones in for larger projects, so as to keep competition alive. The reason is more often the high price of building materials, both local and imported. *I have, therefore, decided that I shall ask the owners of certain firms to invite the Government to join their enterprise.*

Listed firms to sell at least 51 per cent of shares to government

The first firms I wish to mention are Anros Industries Ltd., Monarch (Zambia) Ltd. and Crittal-Hope (Zambia) Ltd. These three companies dominate the field of window and door frame manufacturing. Although this should have been an ideal situation for proper competition between firms operating in Zambia the reverse has actually happened; prices of metal windows manufactured here are excessively high. I am asking the owners of these companies to give the State at least a 51 per cent interest in their enterprises so as to enable us to control and rationalise their production, to eliminate duplication and to lower their prices.

Again on the building industry, I want to ask some building material merchants to invite the State to take at least 51 per cent of their business so that we can reduce the present fantastically high prices and move into new and more acceptable sources of supply. These companies have failed to do so despite the warnings that they have been given many times in the past. The companies I have in mind are Anglo-African Glass Co. Ltd., P.G. Timbers, Baldwins Ltd., Steel Supplies of Zambia Ltd., Zamtimbia Ltd., May and Hassell (Zambia) Ltd., and Johnson and Fletcher. When taken over these companies will operate in conjunction with the State's Zambia Steel and Building Supplies Ltd., wholly owned by the Industrial Development Corporation.

A third group connected with the building industry that I intend to ask to give the State a controlling interest are the three quarries that supply crushed stone in the Lusaka area. They are Nicholas Quarries, Gerry's Quarries and Greystone Quarry. These three quarries have operated an official price ring for many years now through a company called Crushed Stone Sales Ltd. I want the State to take at least 51 per cent of these companies so as to examine the cost of production of such stone which I am advised could be produced for very much less than the price being charged at the moment.

Determination of profit margins of manufacturing industries

Before I move to a new field, I would like to say a few words about prices. It is not only the prices of the construction industry that are high. I am worried about the prices of every type of commodity from foodstuffs to clothing, engineering products, and many others. The Price Control Department has been working hard on the prices of consumer goods mainly. It has been generally preoccupied in fixing retail and wholesale margins for the basic commodities. But my private information tells me that the profit margins of local manufacturers are sky-high. I understand that the manufacturers of clothing, in particular, make so much profit that they pay for their investment in six months. This may be an exaggeration, but I am asking my Minister of Commerce, Industry and Foreign Trade now to look into the profit margins of all the manufacturing industries right through the country, and he must start with the clothing industry.

The next industry where I feel the Government must take an interest is the brewing industry. Northern Breweries Ltd., with its Lusaka subsidiary, and Heinrich's Syndicate Ltd., occupy monopoly positions in their brewing fields. Both these companies are making excessive profits and they could make even more if excessive expenditure on sales promotion were curtailed. I intend to ask both these companies to invite the Government to join in their enterprises to the extent of at least 51 per cent. Their large profits will then be made partly for the nation, which will put them to proper use.

I will now move into the transport field. Transport is of prime importance to our national survival. It is absolutely vital that we rationalise and co-ordinate the activities of our major transport organisations so as to direct them to operate more in the national interest. As you know, rail and air transport is already Government owned and we control Zambia Tanzania Road Services Ltd. The other two big road operators in the country are Smith and Youngson Ltd., and Central African Road Services Ltd. I am asking Central African Road Services Ltd to offer the Government at least 51 per cent of their shares and I am asking Smith and Youngson Ltd. to do the same. It is my intention that when Government has taken over Central African Road Services Ltd., its activities will be confined entirely to passenger transport. In the past the Company has failed to live up to the responsibility of its monopoly position to serve all sections of the community. By engaging in both passenger and freight transport it is running neither properly. I want Smith and Youngson operations to be confined to freight distribution within the country only.

Zambia Railways and Zambia Tanzania Road Services Ltd., will continue to bring goods from abroad. This is the way I want to rationalise the road transport system of the country. At the same time I want to see, as I said earlier, a great number of Zambian businessmen operating buses, taxis, lorries for distribution to the rural areas and so on. So from now on the transport pattern in the country will be three big State controlled organisations assisted by a large number of Zambian operators.

The next field I want the State to engage in is retail and wholesale distribution. As you are aware Government has already, the hard way, set up the Zambia National Wholesale Corporation. This is not enough. Now that I have confined the field of retail trading in many areas and the expansion of retail trading in all places to Zambians, I want to have a retail State organisation operating alongside them so that we have some measure of control over their activities and a check on price inflation. For this reason I am asking certain large retail groups to offer at least 51 per cent of their shares to the Government. These are C.B.C. stores and shops, O.K. Bazaars, Standard Trading, Solanki Brothers Ltd., and Mwaiseni Stores Ltd. When the State has taken over control of these businesses we shall find ways of rationalising their activities so that we will save wasteful duplication where possible.

Earlier on, I referred to the fact that when a Zambian enterprise developed and reached a certain point we would have to make it a public company and when it grew even further the State would have to take it over. Now I have just mentioned a number of retail groups that I have invited to offer their shares to Government. You have no doubt noted that among them is Mwaiseni Stores Ltd. This is a Zambian enterprise which has reached the limit that I have been discussing with you. Indeed, I am a proud man at this moment when I say that Mwaiseni Stores Ltd. has given us a first-class example. This wholly Zambian owned enterprise has readily offered its services in the field of management as well. We will depend on this and one other* which has also agreed to co-operate. This one, although not Zambian as such, is also a firm that has done very well in its Zambianisation programme. However, an announcement will be made about this firm sooner or later. This almost completes the list of companies in which I feel the Government must take a share. But, before I leave this subject I must mention three others. One is Zambezi Sawmills Ltd. where the State will also wish to take at least 51 per cent interest. This company provides the only major employment in an important corner of the country, the Barotse Province, and the present shareholders have several times threatened to close it down.

Another is the Mining Timbers Ltd., which supplies logs and mining poles to the Mines. I also want the State to take at least 51 per cent of the shares of this company. When this is done we should find ways of rationalising the activities of these two companies in order to ensure continued employment in Barotse Province and better utilisation of our timber.

---

*C.B.C. (Zambia), Ltd.

The third one is Zambia Newspapers Ltd. which publishes Zambia's only daily and only Sunday newspapers. It is not right that these major means of informing the public should be under foreign control. I would be happier if at least 51 per cent of Zambia Newspapers Ltd. were in State ownership. I do not intend that newspapers should be operated by Information Department nor do I wish them to be run by State Company. I am anxious under democracy and humanism to create some national body of truly Zambian organisation which will operate these newspapers. I don't want, I repeat countrymen, to confine all important media of communication to government. This would be wrong if we are to build strong democracy here and we aim at doing that. We must allow these newspapers to be in other hands but those hands must be Zambian. Such an organisation, as I say, must be Zambian but divorced from the Government.

The last company I want to invite to give the State at least 51 per cent of its shares is Irvin and Johnson Ltd. You all know that we intend to exploit to the full our fish resources. For this purpose we announced recently that INDECO has entered into an agreement with a group from Norway to establish an organisation to catch and market fish. This organisation will buy all the fish that our peasant fishermen catch. It will process, freeze and sell it in the shops and the markets. This is a very big scheme designed particularly to assist the rural areas. In future the fishermen will have no problem where to sell their fish, this organisation will be there to buy it. But INDECO has been doing things the hard way and the hard way is always a slow way. Now we are in a hurry. We are not going to wait until new freezing facilities have been installed. Indeed I see no reason why we should wait until new refrigerated trucks have been bought and brought into the country. I want this organisation to operate tomorrow, so I am asking for a merger in advance. I am asking Irvin and Johnson Ltd. to give the State 51 per cent of its shares so as to enable us to start this project immediately and to rationalise the operations and avoid duplication of facilities which result in the drain of our foreign exchange. At the same time I want this organisation to look into something else. As you know, it will have major refrigeration facilities right through the country. It will also have refrigerated trucks moving from the various rural areas to the towns in order to carry fish.

While they are doing that, I want them to look into the possibility of carrying poultry and eggs and even vegetables at the same time. You know very well that since Independence I have been pressing for increased poultry production and increased egg production. This is a home industry which private individuals can engage in and in which co-operatives have aready been successful. I want to ensure that their products will move to the markets freely so that nobody will complain that 'Here I am not able to sell my chickens', or 'Here I am not able to sell my eggs'. Further, I want this organisation to look into the possibility of preserving eggs. There are seasons when there is overproduction of eggs. There are seasons when you cannot find an egg in the country. This is what I want to avoid. I want to make sure that eggs are preserved to last from one season to another.

State participation in business through INDECO

These are the only companies in which the State wishes to participate. I want to say a few words now about the valuation of these shares that will be bought by the State. I must make it very clear that everybody is going to get fair compensation. As you all know, the Government already has a well established business arm in the Industrial Development Corporation—INDECO. INDECO already participates to a greater or lesser degree in some twenty companies in commerce, industry, transport and other fields. These are:

Country Hotels Limited. (Building two hotels, one in Luangwa and one at Kasaba Bay; operating Hotel Lyambi at Mongu; renovating Mansa Inn and intending to operate other hotels in other rural towns.)

Indeco Milling Limited. (Establishing roller mills in Mongu, Mkushi and Mansa, expected to come into production before the end of the year; intending to open a fourth mill in Kabompo in the North Western Province early next year.)

Kabwe Industrial Fabrics Limited. (Establishing a jute mill for the manufacture of grain sacks and hessian in Kabwe.)

Kafue Estate Limited. (Building a new township at Kafue to accommodate employees of the major Kafue industries.)

Mukonchi Tobacco Limited. (Virginia Tobacco farming and training scheme thirty miles north of Kabwe. This company is to be transferred to the Agricultural Development Corporation before the end of the year.)

Nitrogen Chemicals of Zambia Limited. (To produce nitrogenous fertilisers, expected to come into production at the beginning of 1970.)

Rucom Industries Limited. (This company, whose name is an abbreviation for the words 'Rural—Commercial' is establishing bakeries, dry cleaners, and factory premises in Balovale, Mongu, Mansa, Kasama and Chipata. These premises will be leased, together with equipment, to local entrepreneurs who, when they prove successful, will be entitled to buy them on instalments.)

Tazama Pipelines Limited. (Expected to be completed during the second half of this year.)

Zambia Clay Industries Limited. (Producing bricks and clay pipes in Kitwe.)

Zambia Hotel Properties Limited. (Establishing two hotels, one in Lusaka and one in Livingstone, which are expected to come into operation in September and July this year respectively.)

Zambia National Wholesale Corporation Ltd. (Operating consumer goods wholesale shops in each province. The Lusaka, Mkushi, Ndola branches have already opened; Mansa is expected to open early May and Kasama, Chingola, Solwezi, Chipata and Choma the second half of this year.)

Zambia Steel and Building Supplies Limited. (Dealing in steel and building supplies with branches in Ndola and Lusaka.)

Chilanga Cement Limited. (Operating a cement factory at Chilanga and expecting to commission a second factory in Ndola by the end of this year.)

Duncan, Gilbey and Matheson (Zambia) Limited. (Producing and bottling spirits in Zambia.)

Dunlop Zambia Limited. (Establishing a car and truck tyre factory in Ndola.)

Kafironda Limited. (Producing civil explosives in Kafironda, near Mufulira. Already producing A.N.B.A. and expecting to produce conventional explosives in 1970.)

Kafue Textiles of Zambia Limited. (Expected to come into production during the last quarter of this year to produce cloth of various types.)

Zambia-Tanzania Road Services Limited. (Operating freight services from Dar es Salaam to Zambia.)

Zambia Sugar Company Limited. (Producing sugar cane at Nakambala Sugar Estates near Mazabuka, and refining sugar in Ndola.)

Lakes Fisheries of Zambia Limited. (To catch fish from the lakes in Zambia, purchase fish from peasant fishermen, process and market right through Zambia.)

INDECO always aims to manage each of these companies in a proper commercial and businesslike way. Of course, it keeps the national interest in mind all the time. INDECO will also look after the new State participations which I have described today and will run them in the same way.

Compensation for acquired shares on the basis of book value of assets

I shall leave it to INDECO to negotiate values and terms of payment but *I want to make it clear that what they will pay is a fair value represented by the book value. There is no such thing as business goodwill or paying for future profits as far as I am concerned.* I cannot see any reason why we should pay extra for the boom we have ourselves created.

I hope that the companies will agree to State participation in their undertakings. However, I wish to make it perfectly clear that in the event of failure of the negotiations Government will compulsorily acquire the shares in these companies. I anticipate that the partnership between the State and the private sector, which I have outlined, can be brought about by consent, but, whether there is consent or not, I will ensure that this implementation of humanism is brought about.

Acquisition of property by government: amendment of Section 18 of the constitution

Perhaps this is an appropriate time for me to announce that Government has accepted in principle the need to amend that part of the Constitution which relates to the compulsory acquisition of property. As humanists we are dedicated to upholding the protection of fundamental rights and the freedom of the individual. However, property rights must be subject to the common good and to the general interests of the community. The existing section

18 of the Constitution must be examined and replaced by more realistic provisions. Another very important matter is the employees of all these companies in which the State will be taking a share. I want to assure them now, all of them, that their interests will not be ignored. I want them to go back to their jobs tomorrow in the same way as they went yesterday. I want them, in fact, to be proud that in the near future they will be working for the State. But all of them must remember to work hard and to produce more. And even more important they must keep discipline. Existing contracts will be honoured and no employee will suffer. In fact for those who are hard-working and loyal promotion prospects will be much improved.

I hope to address my fellow workers on Labour and Youth Day which is 1st May, 1968, to explain what I see as the role of the Labour Movement in this programme. As I see things, this new challenge goes beyond those of us who are workers in urban areas. This challenge calls for a realisation on the part of those of us who are workers in urban areas that whatever benefits we reap from the action we are taking today it should be used to develop our rural areas. This, however, as I say, I hope to discuss with you all at a later stage.

To go back to my subject—right at the beginning I mentioned four types of business existing in Zambia. I have already dealt with resident expatriate business, Zambian private business and State enterprise. This leaves foreign controlled enterprise which I shall turn to now. Foreign controlled business is very important in Zambia and will continue to be so. All the really large enterprises which do not come in the State sector are foreign controlled. Zambia recognises the importance of attracting foreign capital and the foreign skills that go with it. The economic reforms I have outlined today are not aimed at foreign investors. Anyone who studies my remarks will see that they are not. They are designed to implement in the business world the philosophy of Humanism. First, by giving the Zambian people a chance to make their way against resident expatriates who refuse to become citizens of Zambia and yet continue to enjoy, by exploiting us, our economic boom, and, second, by letting the State and ultimately the common man control the activities of certain types of large-scale business and share in its rewards.

Protection of foreign investments

Foreign investors and foreign businessmen are welcome in Zambia. I want to announce straight away that it is my intention to enact legislation safeguarding approved foreign investments. This Foreign Investments Protection Act will provide that a foreign controlled company which is to be established here from a certain date may get a certificate from the Government which will guarantee among other things: that due dividends and interest payments on foreign capital may be remitted abroad; that repatriation of capital brought in from abroad will be allowed; that no expropriation will occur for a set number of years; that any nationalisation thereafter will be at a fair valuation, the method of which shall be laid down in the certificate.

Mining companies

A very special place among the foreign controlled companies operating in Zambia is held by the mining companies. To these I now wish to turn. I am sure they are wondering what their role is in these economic reforms. I do not wish to go into much detail about the mining companies. But there is one step of the greatest importance the Government intends to take and I shall mention it briefly.

Minimal mining development since attainment of Independence

First of all, I want to say to the mining companies that I am very disappointed at the virtual lack of mining development since Independence. Apart from very small developments at Kalengwa and Mimbula Fitula and some further development at existing mines, we have seen nothing. The companies claim that the royalty system has been against new development. Nevertheless I think they have not done enough towards further development of the country in which they make their great profits. Let me also say that I do not agree with the Mining Companies that Royalties have been the obstacle to the development of the Industry. I have been following their accounts and I know very well that they could have embarked upon further expansion if they chose to devote part of their profits for this purpose. Instead of reinvesting they have been distributing over 80 per cent of their profits every year as dividends.

Mining development: new 'mineral royalty' system

However, I am going to change the royalty system. I cannot announce details yet but I can say that the new system will give the Government the same money while it will meet the Companies' point of view. But at the same time I want to see more of those locally made profits utilised in mining development. I do not want to see 80 per cent or 90 per cent of the profits go abroad in the form of dividends. As from today the maximum that the Mining Companies will be allowed to remit abroad in dividends is only half of their profits. The other half they must utilise for further development.

Amendment of exchange control regulations

This policy will apply not only to the Mining Companies but to all foreign-controlled companies which operate in Zambia whichever field they operate in—commerce, industry, agriculture, etc. From now on the exchange control regulations will be amended to allow them to remit dividends abroad only when those dividends do not exceed 30 per cent of the equity capital of the companies provided that the 30 per cent does not exceed half of their profits. In other words, if they make profits they can send half of them to their shareholders abroad but if that half means that their shareholders abroad are going to get a 100 per cent dividend then they cannot do so because it means that the company is undercapitalised; it means that they brought too little money from overseas and they have borrowed too much locally and therefore they must be made to reinvest it in order to capitalise their companies properly. I am tired of people who bring one Kwacha from overseas and yet want to take out three in the first year and this I intend to stop by these regulations.

I want everybody to know that I want no monkey tricks at all. Comrade, Minister of Transport, Power and Communications; comrade, Minister of Finance; from now on I want you to instruct all your aerodrome officials; the Minister of Home Affairs, I want you to instruct all your officials on borders not to allow any car to go by improperly checked. We shall not from now on allow small planes to take off from our aerodromes without proper checking at all. Remember all tricks they play; tyres, shoes, petticoats, and everything. They move on tricks. The Minister of Finance, the

Minister of Home Affairs, the Minister of Transport, Power and Communications and their Permanent Secretaries must get ready right now. Indeed, I am going to announce that the Minister of Legal Affairs, the Governor of the Bank of Zambia, Permanent Secretary, Ministry of Finance, have been working out these regulations lest some of these people should be mischievous. They are in Lusaka now and a *Gazette* will be issued as soon as possible. We have been watching these actions for three and a half years, every trick, and we will deal with anyone who tries to deceive the country.

Many of the policy decisions which I have announced can be implemented at once; others will require legislation. I am instructing my Ministers to ensure that the necessary Acts and Regulations are enacted into law as speedily as possible.

Need for loyalty, hard work, sacrifice and self-reliance

Comrades, Friends and Countrymen, the steps we take today are not in themselves a cure for our economic problems in the country. No doubt used properly they will go a long way towards solving a number of our problems. However, let me emphasise the fact that the State taking control of a number of important firms is not a substitute for sacrifice, hard work and self-reliance on our part. I repeat now, perhaps more than ever before, we must call for loyalty, hard work and honesty on the part of each and every Zambian who believes in Humanism.

Countrymen, let each one of you here understand and appreciate and, indeed, through you all our people in the country, that the measures we take today do not mean fat cheques today, tomorrow or the following year. Whatever we reap from these measures must be put together to enable us to push for economic development in those parts of our country where we have little or no economic development. Who among us here does not know that the order of nature is that we have got to cultivate, sow and weed before we harvest? At this point in time, we are just cultivating. Planting will be our next step and then, of course, the inevitable weeding and thereafter harvesting and we hope rejoicing. Between this period of cultivating and harvesting will be a number of obstacles. The time will come for tightening of belts, as I have said before. State control is completely meaningless without the basic understanding on our part that this is designed to help us hasten the day when each and every Zambian has plenty to eat, decent clothes to wear and a decent shelter to live in. For, I ask again, what is economic activity about? Is it not about MAN? If we understand the depth of this matter every Zambian must decide now what part he is to play in bringing about this goal.

Investing for future development

If I may emphasise the point by giving yet a few more examples, this whole exercise is designed to help reconstruct and one way in which this is to be done is to keep some of the profits, which at the moment go out, within the country. These profits can be used as capital to start up new industries where our people will find employment and thereby occupy themselves usefully. This will also help the reluctant investor get more profits from his new enterprise. In this way he will also contribute to the process of stabilising the country. In other words, I am emphasising the fact that most of the funds that we reap from this action will be used in opening up our rural areas. We also hope that this measure will help us to bring down the cost of living.

Economic revolution: need for public participation

There is yet another point I must emphasise and this is that just as our political revolutionary movement was successful only because of its mass movement character the economic revolution that we believe in, which by definition is one that affects all our people, will never take off without massive support for it. Massive support does not come about by accident. It comes about by a carefully well-thought-out plan which must be effected or implemented through an equally carefully planned administration and organisation. This is why I said earlier on in my introductory remarks that I wanted to see all of us in the country at various levels, especially political and Civil Service wings of the Nation, become more active at both the Provincial and District levels. If we are to succeed this is the only thing that makes sense. I hope we will definitely be able to discuss this aspect of our Development Plan. I am not saying: apportion blame on any one section at all. I am saying: check on the bottlenecks and see how we can really get moving. Here, too, I repeat we will have a few funds for reinvestment in the country and I do hope that those responsible will not need to be coerced but that they will co-operate of their own free will.

Co-operatives: the basis of economic life in Zambia

Yet another point I would like to stress is that I do want to see economic life grow in the country on the basis of co-operatives. Co-operatives could meet future needs that State-controlled enterprises will not be able to meet whether it is in retail, transport or construction fields. This is the surest way in which we can bring back the village-type spirit of co-operation that is so desirable in the reconstruction of this country. When I speak of co-operation I do not want us to tie the nation to anything dogmatic at all. I want us to experiment with various types of co-operatives in accordance with the desires and will of the People under the collective leadership of the Party. Let the People be the judges, whether it is in politics or economics. No doubt mistakes will be made by them but if they are properly guided they will learn from their own mistakes. Again it is the question of trial and error.

Comrades, Friends and Countrymen, what I am saying, emphasised in another way, is we must believe in the power of collective leadership; but even this is only sufficient if in the end we respect and believe in the only safe repository of power which is the people from among whom the common man emerges. We must believe that this is as true economically as it is politically. We must believe that economic power can only belong to the people if we work the co-operative way in every field of economic endeavour. We must believe that where the co-operative endeavour is not possible the State must play its role. The State can either do this directly, or by allowing private enterprise to undertake the task in conjunction with the State or by itself in accordance with the policy laid down in *Humanism in Zambia*. This, in other words, is a realisation of our limits in certain fields and is an acceptance of the importance of combining idealism with realism.

At the beginning of this economic programme each one of us here must play our part in preparing ourselves and those that we represent in this great task of shouldering heavier economic responsibilities collectively.

Commending economic programme to the nation

Comrade Vice-President, Comrades National Councillors, Guests and Friends; in the name of the Almighty God, our Creator, He who was not mistaken to provide for us His children so much potential, He who continues to bless this our young country in the face of so many enemies and obstacles within as well as outside the country; indeed in the name of the people He has directed that we should serve for a time; in the name of the brave people who fought and sacrificed all that they had so that we should be independent; in the name of the Zambian posterity whose interest it falls to us to safeguard at this particular point in time, I commend to you all this economic programme.

May God bless you.

4

HUMANISM AND MONEY IN ZAMBIA

Justin B Zulu*

Introduction

Economics has been defined as "the study of human behaviour as a relationship between ends and means which have alternative uses". We, however, consider this theoretical and functional conception as falling far short of the real task, the scope and the study of economics. It is too restrictive and too sure, and we must suspect anything which sounds too certain. We would therefore suggest that one of the greatest scholars and students of Economics, Alfred Marshall, defined the science most adequately when he said:

> POLITICAL ECONOMY or ECONOMICS is a study of mankind in the ordinary business of life; it examines that part of individual and social action which is most closely connected with the use of the material requisites of wellbeing.

> Thus it is on the one side a study of wealth; and on the other, and more important side, a part of the study of Man.[1]

Hence the present exercise on humanism and money can be regarded, to be pompous, as an introduction to the study of man and wealth in the Zambian context. From Alfred Marshall's insight and prevision we can safely draw the conclusion that there is an economic rationale for humanism and vice versa. This essay therefore draws for intellectual inspiration and frame of reference upon an accurate abstraction from social reality of a most eminent economist; and whatever are the obvious shortcomings of the exercise they are our own. We will thus attempt briefly to elaborate humanism and money and examine the functional relationship

*Dr. Justin B. Zulu, Governor of the Bank of Zambia, was formerly Permanent Secretary in the Office of National Development and Planning.
1. Alfred Marshall, *Principles of Economics* (Macmillan & Co., 1890).

between them as well as the images and realities of that relationship in the real life context of individual persons, business units and Government.

The World of Man and Money

In the thirteenth century or thereabouts, man was considered to be at the centre of the universe: the rationale being partly in the belief that the earth was at the centre of the universe, and partly in a rather generous belief in science, its predictive powers, and its potential to provide mankind with all the answers. If mankind applied the method of science, it was said, he would wield ultimate control over physical matter, and banish mystery from the universe. Whatever has been proved or disproved by subsequent historical developments this was clearly a profound belief in man. It was belief in man as some kind of prime mover, as a means for action, and as an instrument of change.

Zambian humanism goes a step further. It draws for its sustenance not only upon science and its unlimited possibilities, but also upon religion. It is, however, without the exclusiveness of the one and the institutionalisation of the other. It is therefore larger than religion; larger than the familiar partisan ideological systems or stances. In short, Zambian humanism is an act of faith, a profound belief in man. Man is not only at the centre of society, but also at its growing apex; man is not only a means for economic action, but also a setting for that action; man is not only an instrument of economic change, but also an end for the change. It therefore seeks to recognise and reconcile this characteristic duality of man. A confrontation with his own duality must place upon him great responsibility; it is a therapy he tends to ignore, or indeed avoid at his own peril and that of the society of which he is a member. In practical economics humanism simply urges that each man, no matter what station of life, shall take full part both in the decision and action to produce and in the decision and action to distribute the aggregate social and economic product. This is a great challenge, but also, and this is most important, a great opportunity for any young nation.

In a world of less and less practical use for precedent, living is a continuum of collisions with day-to-day reality. There is disease; there is poverty; there is ignorance; there is social injustice; there is rapid commercialisation of values; the nuclear holocast hangs over man's head like the sword of Damocles. There is the growing insecurity of the individual in inverse relationship to the growing pressures and needs of the group; change is the rule rather than the exception. These are survival problems, and therefore economic as well as social. Somehow, somewhere, we can sense an undercurrent of the familiar problems of choice, of scarcity of resources, of allocation, of misallocation, of values in a state of flux, or lack of control and direction of the forces unleashed by the processes of 'progress'.

It is not easy to crystallise into everyday functional attributes something as unquantifiable as humanism; nonetheless, it may suffice to give it one breakdown. A sample list would probably go like this: magnanimity; an inclusive vision of life; wearing others' boots; goodwill; remembering the underprivileged; kindness and love; integrity; social justice; a sense of human purpose . . . The sky is the limit! There are probably three common features about them: they are rather nebulous, and suggest attitude, states of mind, outlook, and atmosphere; secondly, they are not hurricanes or tornadoes; they are not popular movements or powerful forces, rather private and unhistoric little acts; thirdly, for mankind as a whole, they constitute some sort of *consensus gentium*—a general sense of agreement about human values. They promise no immediate reward to Mr. A or Mr. B, no crowns of laurel, yet the incidence of good, or of personal security, or of social continuity or of voluntary productivity or of social cohesion in any given society or community depends upon them.

The present world, therefore, has a practical use for the virtues just described. They oil the machine . . . soothe the nerves of a frantic generation . . . smooth out human relations . . . upgrade the human condition and enlarge upon the quality of life and its expectations. By life in this exercise we mean that which moves onwards; that which exists and grows by itself and by everything which it touches; that which responds productively and positively to any stimulus. The virtues therefore are an integral part of day-to-day economic and social activity, be it at the individual level or the business enterprise level or the government level.

Let us now turn to money. Marshall described economic resources as "material requisites of wellbeing"; the operative words are clearly 'requisite' and 'wellbeing', be it material or spiritual or aesthetic. Wellbeing is a requisite for human life *per se* and for the human struggle as expressed through the application of knowledge and the ordering of natural resources for purposes of production. At the abstract level money may be related to its value for purposes of the exchange of goods and services. But its value at any time is not guaranteed, rather it depends upon the comparative productivities of persons, groups, societies, or countries involved in economic exchange. Behind the productivities are many factors; here it is sufficient to point out that the value of money is also a function of operational, attitudinal, and historical factors. For instance, the international monetary system and its payments infrastructure, are delicately balanced on the tightrope of mutual international trust. No ordinary decision-maker is required or expected to comprehend money beyond its functions as a measure of value and store of wealth. Nor is it necessary for him to agonise over recurring press headlines such as "the gold flow" or "flight of gold" or "the gold crisis".

For the average decision-maker money is a practical commodity; this is what matters and what concerns us most here. Money should therefore be defined very broadly to mean and include: income, wages, the price level, interest, rent, profits, bills of exchange, promissory notes, overdrafts, investment, credit cards, loans, letters of credit, foreign exchange, etc. This is not the conventional definition of money supply: here we are interested in money as a means or instrument of economic and social action. The mixed-bag characteristic of modern money reflects the complex payments system which has developed out of experience, and for the convenience of man. Each kind represents both a payment and a receipt. Take the wages: from the point of view of the employer wages are a payment and an outflow, while from that of an employee they are a receipt.

The vested interests or motives behind each transaction are normally not identical. They may be influenced by many contractual and institutional factors, and also by attitudes including what each party considers the right exchange value for the rôle he is playing. However, either by design or coincidence, the interest groups constitute a self-contained mixed bag of economic action and reaction. And from the operational angle the bag is a forum of a continuous economic and social dialectic, and a system for identifying and reconciling the economic and social capacities, as well as claims and counterclaims in a modern exchange economy.

Probably, the most important feature which readily emerges out of the situation just described is *Dependence*. The scope of dependence between man and man increases rather than declines with increased economic and social sophistication. The sophistication is engendered partly by increased functional specialisation; and specialisation means vastly increased human interaction with all its implications for human relations and values.

This exchange system does not in reality mirror an elaborate economic and social clearing-house for payments and receipts or for claims and counterclaims by impersonal forces and institutions. Rather it is a forum portraying the activities of real life producers and consumers; therefore each payment or receipt is a means to an end. The immediate end might be profit, or wages, or fees, or investment; the intermediate end might be production, or it might be consumption, or both. But the ultimate end is man himself. The payments, receipts, production and consumption are not once-and-for-all acts. The definition of money must, therefore, be further extended to include both past, present and future values and streams of income. For instance, the size of expected income of an individual, a firm or government has a bearing on present economic behaviour. It will determine how much and how far an economic decision-making unit can commit itself in the present situation.

From the foregoing analysis and observation, money cannot be conceived of only, or mainly, in the physical sense of coins, currency notes, or any of its proliferate substitutes. It must also be conceived of in terms of payments systems, the institutional set-up, accounting procedures, administrative practices and many other communications media. These characteristics bring into play continuous interaction of people, money and technology. A language and systems machine is created which must be properly serviced by positive human attitudes and habits. In this way the impersonal, and the thoroughness of systems and institutions can be minimised, leaving a sufficient margin of freedom for man in his capacity as an individual, or as businessman, or as the locus of political power and therefore of government.

Doing as you please

In the process of the creation of wealth the individual is both the agent and the beneficiary. There is some kind of dilemma here, not in the sense that he has reached his wit's end or is at the crossroads. Rather in the sense that he is called upon to accept full responsibility in executing the rôles which are not necessarily complementary. He also gets no consolation from being both a social and economic man. And not infrequently there is a proclivity to see an inherent dichotomy between what is spiritual and what is material. A little reflection shows that these compartments are essentially states of mind, images rather than realities. It is true man is a mixed bag, but of integral parts, and therefore a single entity which cannot be compartmentalised. It is true also that he is both object and subject. And in order to operate in any human activity he must initially grapple with his own dualism; to be able to do so he must have the will and the means. First, with the help of science and technology he can substantially reduce physical drudgery, disease, ignorance; and substantially increase the benefits of leisure, education, culture, consumption and opportunity. Money too should be regarded as a means, a tool, a gadget; like any piece of technology which is primarily for the improvement of the quality of life.

Secondly, technology must be made accessible to the greatest number for the greatest good; and must be an adjunct to man in the process of shaping the environment. By technology we do not simply imply physical gadgets and computors. We also refer to systems, habits, expectations, attitudes, and behaviour resulting from today's sense of urgency or today's sense of time ("time is money"), and to the many logistics and gimmicks deployed today for doing things 'better' and more efficiently. The more widely available the better; the strains of technological inequality are lessened, so are those which result from great disparity in the enjoyment of its fruits. The same can be said of money. Its function is that of a powerful tool in the hand of Man. This tool is for either creating or upgrading technology (capital formation), or directly for satisfying man's immediate social and physical needs (consumption). Here also the more widely available the better. It is essentially a passive tool; but once in the hands of a decision-maker it can become very much alive. It can be a dangerous or a creative tool; it can be an instrument of death, or of life.

These features and characteristics described have certain implications. A situation where wealth exists side by side with abject poverty is a menacing one. It creates an unstable co-existence, a hot-bed of tension and friction. A more equitable distribution of economic power is thus vital; but a permanent movement towards its attainment cannot be imposed, or sustained from above, or achieved by impersonal forces without doing damage to a man-centred society. For in such a society private relations, exchanges, relationships, reactions, associations and even inhibitions are indispensable. They constitute the voluntary and spontaneous effort which, if allowed expression, must influence economic patterns and trends. Government can then assume the task of preparing the stage and providing the requisite maintenance, as will be indicated later in this paper.

In short, each individual is given not only a challenge but also an opportunity to assume a more productive role in the labour market, or consumer market, or capital market. In this way his flow of income and consumption should more or less reflect his comparative productivity. In a planned economy, serving the State may be the sole purpose of production; in a free enterprise one, material success may be the motivating factor. In a man-centred society, while neither the State nor personal success is irrelevant, the beneficiary should directly be man *per se*. *Individuals and other decision-makers can and should accumulate material wealth so long as the manner of acquisition or utilisation does not lead to stunted personal growth.*

An honest contribution, however humble, to the net growth of the social product is expected of every man and woman. President Kaunda, at the close of his essay on *Humanism in Zambia*, points out very succinctly that laziness or disinclination to hard work or lack of purpose in a man-centred society is a form of exploitation. A society which aims at respecting all men whatever their station in life has its own rules; failure by any individual to live up to the rules of the game must be regarded as a serious betrayal to the society. The menacing situation where extreme poverty and great wealth confront each other across a firing line is repeated when hard work and laziness are in confrontation. A firing line is created, not between the haves and have-nots this time, but between the resourceful and the truant. No two individuals have the same drive, nor the same productive capacities. This is recognised not only because it is a fact of human experience, but also because of the rich and unlimited variety which character-ises the nature and distribution of human capacity and talent.

Consequently, a man-centred society must protect and promote all kinds of talent. The protection of the resourceful is not only for their benefit but also, and even more important, for the promotion of resourcefulness itself. There must be no let-up in the task of raising the general average of human performance. Where wholesome initiative is denied either expression or recognition deviant social behaviour finds root and individuals may be compelled to put self before society. An individual can choose an honest good day's work in somebody's employment. A man can use his own natural or acquired latent for a debut in the dizzy world of the creative arts. He can use his initiative to organise one or more factors of production in order to create wealth. He can provide a service, he can provide a good; it is left to the individual to choose. All that humanism insists upon, and expects of each individual, is that he commit himself to producing or creating something which will be of direct or indirect economic and social benefit to himself and to the society of which he is a vital unit.

Any serious and sustained contribution must be preceded by proper and sufficient preparedness. In the first place each individual should more accurately assess himself, his powers and his abilities. This is a step which is often overlooked, or to which little attention is paid, with dire consequences. In other words, the emphasis in a man-centred society is less on emulating the next-door neighbour, or group, or the other people, than directing one's energies to what one can actually do, given the personal potentialities, plus the real rather than the imagined constraints in the immediate environment. Such a society does not come about by preaching or listening to the preaching, however effective or thorough. It is not an idea in the clouds; it is not a philosophy or an ideology. Rather it is a field job.

In the field the rôle of the individual in harmonising humanism and material wealth is not merely confined to accurate knowledge of the right priorities of self-development, and greater involvement. There must also be a practical commitment to achieving these and other goals. Income disposal needs to be guided by a certain priority scale of values. At the top of the scale is investment in more permanent self-improvement. The common man should continuously increase his ability to adapt to the swift and incessant change taking place in his environment. Self-improvement is also necessary in order to minimise the natural wear and tear, aesthetic or spiritual, or physical. The disposable income will therefore be channelled into increasing sensitivity, sharpening response, and last but not least maintaining his market value in an economy beleaguered by technological unemployment. The initiative must be engendered from within; the individual must have a rational basis for understanding the change which has occurred to him and around him; such private knowledge and private feeling in a man-centred society are indispensable.

Next on the priority scale must come the development of other people: the family unit, the immediate community and the greater society. For the individual this is the surest way of funding the quality of life achieved so far, or to be achieved. The quality of life of the greater part of the society must be rising too or else there is created a "drag effect" on the resourceful. Everybody benefits more from being a member of a generally more wealthy society, or a generally more healthy society, or a generally more educated and enlightened one. In a nutshell, proper and adequate capitalisation of the human machine is as important as that of a business partnership, a statutory body, a co-operative society, a public company, or a government.

All this points out to the inalienable importance of the individual. In his capacity as an economic and social agent, he must have proper and satisfying avenues for self-expression. Like economic needs, social needs are unlimited, varied, sometimes complementary, and at other times conflicting. On the other hand, social resources are by some law of Providence characteristically scarce. The means for converting scarce resources into goods and services, and the means for shaping the environment, have also become increasingly complex and sophisticated. Man must therefore operate under pressure, to discover, devise, perfect as well as harness them in a race against time.

Human life is therefore a practical business. When you come across a fellow human being with a fractured limb in a hit-and-run traffic accident it is not enough merely to feel sorry and express sentiments of concern. What the victim really needs in this moment of agony is practical help. He needs first-aid assistance; he needs transportation to the nearest hospital; he needs a doctor's attention. These and many more are practical logistics involving some know-how, decision-making, physical energy, and indeed money (a car or a bicycle, a stretcher, a telephone SOS . . .) Similarly, not infrequently one comes across a striken group of fellow humans. They have had no rains, or their fields or livestock have been destroyed by a freak storm, a heat-wave, a tornado, a hurricane, floods, accidental fire, an earthquake or a bombing raid! Sadly enough all these are familiar matters of today. Is it not a spontaneous reaction to organise practical help: food, medicine, shelter, water, sanitation, transportation, rescue gear? Money therefore has been one of man's best friends in alleviating human tribulation and anguish.

Thus, in searching for the rôle of the individual we have attempted, though imperfectly, to state that he should continuously seek to increase his freedom. Later in this exercise we will state that he needs assistance in this task. By freedom we do not mean 'doing as you please'; we also do not mean the opposite of determinism, nor the synonym of anarchy. By freedom we mean increased presence of mind or productive capacity, or creative power as a human being, in order to matter, and in order to have significance. This is vital, in a man-centred society a man or woman must be an asset rather than a liability both in the small and the great decisions and purposes of that society.

A business is in business

The apparent immediate objective of a business enterprise or businessman is to make a quick return out of his investment. In order to do this he must operate in at least three markets directly or indirectly, namely—labour, capital goods, and final product. He is only one of many operating in the same markets; the fellow operators have no immediate identical motives or interests. If he is producing a good or service he must employ fellow human beings as well as his own or other people's savings. It is therefore a co-operative exercise from the outset, and from the outset a continuous human interaction. In the whole operation man is the vital means whether he is the dustman or the executive director of the company.

Therefore, the process of creating money or creating a good, or providing a service, or organising factors of production, can be motivated by many factors. It can for instance be motivated by immediate material benefit. While this is legitimate, man is not a mere adjunct to profit. On a metaphysical plane man in the act of social and economic production is seen as extending himself

beyond his physical point in time and place. He does so in project-
ing his image on physical matter and manipulating it in order to
satisfy his needs. Production is therefore symbolic of man participating as fully as possible in the process of continuously shaping
and reshaping his environment.

On the economic plane the picture is not very different. The
narrow reason for being of business, normally called profit, is more
and more a feature of the past; individuals in an increasingly larger
sector of modern business also want to maximise other desires.
Some top executives want to maximise self-development, they
can then become sort of professional directors of boards. In some
cases the attainment of success in a particular business is regarded
as a requisite stepping-stone for eligibility for bigger and better
positions in bigger business concerns. Sometimes it is preferable
to maximise the volume of sales rather than profit per unit. Sometimes it is more important to retain existing markets or win new
ones in place of a large instant profit. In other cases personal success
in business management becomes identified with personal success
in life. Indeed modern research has confirmed and revealed that a
large number of hours, and a good deal of human ingenuity
are invested every year in maximising business achievement for
motives other than quick profit. There is therefore a business
rationale behind humanism and vice versa. Small wonder that the
exercise of business social responsibility has increased out of all
recognition compared to the human condition in the "satanic
mills" of the Industrial Revolution. Humanism seeks to accelerate
it further and to make it a permanent feature of business ethics
and business practice.

Social responsibility can be related to the quality of customer
service provided. This may sound rather too obvious to point out,
except that customer service here has a broader definition; it takes
into account the rôles of the customer as well as the producer.
It is not only the production of shoddy goods and provision of inadequate service which are at stake—this is only one side of the
coin. On the other side is shoddy workmanship. What subtracts
from human quality must in the end subtract from the quality
of the goods and services produced and distributed. Customer
service is only one example of unlimited opportunities for the
abuse or the exercise of social responsibility. Also, social responsibility does not come about by itself, it has to be cultivated.

For instance, owners or organisers of the means of social and economic production must properly and adequately capitalise their enterprises. This is particularly important in developing economies. Adequate capitalisation implies greater commitment of risk capital, for this is the main justification for choosing an economic order which also permits voluntary effort and initiative. An economy which is sustained by debt has weak foundations; sooner or later a time must come when the servicing of debt is greater than the inflowing capital. The proclivity of living beyond one's means is objectionable, alike for government, individuals and businesses.

Sometimes business practice is motivated by shortsighted logistics. One such example is where the aim is to secure a monopolistic situation. There is nothing improper in cornering a market on grounds of lower unit costs, or on grounds of economic efficiency, or when the benefits are also passed on to the consumer. But more often than not this is not the case, and a cornered market may be a great opportunity, and it may be a curse. In the latter situation the temptation is often reflected in overpricing, in shoddy workmanship, in shoddy customer service, even inappropriate sales pressures. Such practices place the consumer at the tender mercy of a perverted version of the profit motive, and they give the impression that the conduct of business is inherently ruthless and inhuman. In reality business is essentially an activity of human beings, by human beings and for human beings.

The process of adding utilities of form, time and place is a challenge and an opportunity to business ingenuity. Forests, water, rock, grass, soil, air, land, weather, climate have been transformed into one form of wealth or another. In all these efforts the profit motive is essentially a mere by-product when looked at from the sum total of human achievement. Among the real products which are never readily apparent to the entrepreneur or to the ordinary eye are two impacts. One is the creation of an entirely new physical environment. Look at the towering skyscrapers, or the incessant battle of neon signs at night, or the criss-crossing modern highways, or the vast amounts of synthetic products, and indeed at the vast possibilities of creating and sustaining life as well as annihilating it from the face of the earth! The second is a corollary to the symbols of genius just described: it is man's absolute determination for survival. However, in the ensuing 'rat race' individual and private accomplishments may pass unnoticed; or the immediate benefit may accrue only to the decision-maker concerned. Nevertheless, it is the millions of such 'inconsequential' private accomplishments which upgrade the social and economic environment. Indeed, it is not necessary for a society to plan for the production of geniuses. What is really critical is spreading the enlightenment and creative response of the general population, so that when a genius is born he and his work can be more readily recognised. Money is one of the means for creating such an atmosphere and enviromment.

Apart from working for himself and for society as a whole, the businessman must be deeply conscious of his vital rôle; he can then enlarge upon his assumptions and his motives. The cynic may argue that a 'business is in business', and it must make profit in order to stay there. This assertion cannot be denied nor ignored, but it can be examined and enriched. If the 'business is in business' philosophy is inspired by the theory of the survival of the fittest, then it is governed by images rather than realities. In a world under constant threat of nuclear disaster or moral dilemma the problem is essentially one of the survival of Man himself, rather than of the fittest. We all want security, stability, certainty, but more often than not there appears to be a great deal of confusion as to what constitutes security. If any businessman, or machinist, or night-watchman, or trade unionist, should think the answer is in money, or in social position, or in some form of power, he would be shocked to read the case histories of physicians and psychiatrists. Their private rooms are crowded with men and women who could corner the market on happiness if money or power could buy that commodity. Behind the facade of wealth, or beautiful clothes, or power or the fanfare of high society, there is also widespread 'quiet desperation'.

At this point it is proper to state the underlying assumptions to our comment on business ethics. First, although on the surface a firm can be defined as a business unit with separate legal existence, it is in reality a social organism—a complex interaction not so much of machines, or production processes, but rather of men and women. Second, the growing separation of ownership and control in modern business organisation has many implications. The most important is that there is in reality no 'boss', all are actually employees from the top executive right down to the dustman. Third, because a firm is essentially a social organisation it is also a custodian of values. The values reflect the society's generally

prevalent inner tensions, and attitudes to hard work, initiative, efficiency, leisure, social responsibility and workmanship among others.
Management, therefore, involves to a large extent direction and control of people, which is essentially different from direction and control
of materials, processes, procedures, and flow charts. Fourth,
managers cannot be mere efficiency engineers; they cannot
think merely in terms of costs, or returns, or prices, or output
levels. Regular maintenance of machines has to be matched with
social security schemes and regular provision of safety measures
as well as health services. Regular replacement of fixed capital or
movable plant has to be matched by retraining programmes for
the work force.

Finally, the business unit must endeavour to preserve its identity
in the face of increasing social control over social and economic
production. To do this it is necessary to have an informed assessment and grasp of the major changes taking place. First, it is
important for a business concern to know that differentials between pay rates are of more significance in the social structure of
an enterprise than the pay rates themselves. Second, it is important
to know that productivity is more a function of the quality of
management attitude and technique than of labour attitudes.
Third, it is important to know that in an increasingly employee
society, wages and salaries are social status symbols. Fourth, it
is also important to know that with the increasing application of
technology the proportion of direct to indirect labour is fast declin-
ing and fast losing significance. Accurate measurement of the
contribution of direct labour to social and economic production is
thus impossible, and so is accurate assessment of the share due
to direct labour. The right social and economic measures can then
be formulated and implemented by the enterprise itself. Such action
will tend to reduce the need for government action or commissions
of enquiry, or strike action in bringing about economic justice.

Opportunity and opportunity of access

We pointed out that in the creation and utilisation of wealth
the individual and business firm are at one and the same time
agents as well as direct beneficiaries. The position with regard
to government in this matter is slightly different. Being impersonal,
government can take long- or short-term decisions of a general nature
with or without immediate benefits to itself. True, once in the

seat of power, government has a propensity to develop vested interest in itself. Like any vulnerable or living organism it will instinctively seek self-perpetuation or some other form of immortality. However, be that as it may, in a man-centred society the overall primary function of government is to protect and stimulate areas of voluntary productive effort and initiative in that society. By areas of voluntary productive effort and initiative we mean individuals, partnerships, private companies, co-operatives, professional associations and social institutions, to mention only a few. It is precisely these areas of private and voluntary activity and association which are the cradle of creativity, initiative, and purpose, and the cradle of impulses which have placed man at the apex of the scheme of creation.

A government which is committed to humanism will envisage the evolution of an egalitarian society in material wellbeing. While this is a realistic and honourable objective, it is rather narrow. Material egalitarianism is hardly original; goods and services are a necessary but not sufficient reason for being of a society or a government. A man-centred society will go further than physical survival of man; it will accord sufficient priority to the formulation and implementation of development plans in non-material wealth. The primary strategy therefore is the development of the citizens themselves, i.e. their social as well as economic skills. By social skills we mean, among other things, culture, education, aesthetics, recreation, entertainment, social responsibility and a sense of public service. Where these social skills are sufficiently cultivated and integrated, the attitudes to material wealth are generally broad and mature; money is not the end, nor the driving force underlying personal striving or human existence. Secondly, regarding the rough road of 'rags to riches' the end does not justify the means. Thirdly, in the day-to-day life conspicuous consumption scores low on the priority scale of values. If it has been possible to invest vast sums of money and foreign exchange in tangible goods and services, it could not be more vital to invest as much in the human attitudes, habits, and expectations which will produce a more balanced citizen.

The level of social skills is critical also from another consideration. The failure of many an economic policy or plan can be partly, if not mainly, attributed to social inertia. Inadequate attention tends to be paid to social response by planners and policy makers.

This perennial oversight of the potential rôle of social reaction is not merely a matter of ignorance, or of technical negligence, but also of the preoccupation with econometric modelling. Instinctively, in a world of increasing classification, measurement, categorisation and quantification of human experience, areas which cannot pass this test—the proclivity for intellectual certainty—tend to be regarded as given.

Last, but not least, the social skills listed are more than skills in the narrow sense of the term; they are attributes of human personality. They have the effect of sensitising the social, cultural, and aesthetic potential of the individual human beings. This process enlarges the surface of individual contact with other human beings, with nature, with the man-made environment, and with the physical world in general. Once the surface of contact is enlarged individuals develop a richer sense of judgement; they become more tolerant; they are more aware of the human potential as well as the human limitation; they develop a larger heart and kindlier hand, and not infrequently a more creative personal style. Armed with such humility their frame of reference is sharpened, so are their expectations from life, and their potential contribution. An exposure of the greatest number of the citizens to such influences at government expense must ultimately pay out the highest social and economic dividends.

By economic skills we mean, among other things, technical training, professional attainment, employment opportunity, manual labour, management and other specialised forms of training or work experience. The significance of these skills in a modern economy needs no elaboration. They have a direct bearing on the labour market, on the physical goods market, as well as on man's desire to tame the natural elements and convert whatever is therein into economic resources. Technological progress is sustained by them. On the reverse side of the coin, the skills are themselves under great pressure from changing technology, changing business organisation and method, and changing job classification. There is also the pressure from the ever-growing inventiveness of the industrial technocrats in the attempt to reduce unit costs or create new markets, and the ingenuity of the workers themselves as a logical by-product of the job experience.

These are essentially pressures on the durability, quality, and adaptability of social and economic skills. An environment comes into being whereby new skills are created as rapidly as the old ones become obsolete. Such a situation, whether created by environmental upheavals, or by man himself in the attempt to stabilise his own spiritual and physical bearings, tend to create a loss of significance. At the same time, money capital, land, technology, labour, are in some sense passive; left to themselves they cannot bring about production. They have to be harnessed, channelled and transformed into usable instruments. The task of managing these resources, and adding to them the utilities of form, time and place falls squarely on man, either as a single individual or man in a group, or man in an association, or man in an institution.

It is therefore proper that the second overall strategy of government is the laying down of a social and economic infrastructure. In this context, infrastructure is defined loosely to mean adequate provision of the functional institutional set-up. It might also be spelt out as follows: health services, education, training centres, roads, tax provisions, business law, law and order, telecommunications, national security, banking system, social and community services, local government, information service, research, social security schemes, power and energy and transport systems. These structures, or utilities or institutions, contribute to the pace and quality of economic and social change at any given time. They provide a frame of reference, a point of departure, social, economic, as well as administrative. Their durability and utility is derived from their capacity to be adapted to changing circumstances, and in a man-centred society they are and must remain adjuncts to man rather than man to them.

However, it is not enough to provide an economic and social infrastructure. Decision-making units must have the opportunity of access to them. This is another primary strategy of government. Access means, among other things, that the structures provided are immediately relevant to the consumers and users; that they are convenient in terms of form, time and place; that they are tailored to the capacities of the consumers and users while leaving sufficient room to stretch or challenge them. Thus problems of production, employment, distribution and of development in general, are too important to be left to find their own level. Social unrest or discontent can undermine, even nullify, any hard-won economic transformation. It is important therefore to see not only that a "land of opportunity" is brought into being by the government, but also that that opportunity is accessible to the vast majority of the population.

However, it must be pointed out that opportunity of access, where it exists, is only part of the background, which may be one vast mosaic of many other wares also on display. The incentive for a vendor to continue to market his product is sustained by the profit margin, or by the other business objectives described earlier, or by the desirability of the product as expressed through the volume of demand for it. Government is in a similar situation with regard to its wares. A given service or situation can be an opportunity to person or decision-maker A, and yet be nothing of the sort to B. Admittedly, opportunities are not uniformly distributed; but response must be assessed on how each person or body of persons positively responds to whatever mix or size of existing opportunity; humanism places the onus of development on man rather than on obstacles. It is therefore necessary but not sufficient for the State to provide or create opportunities. The individuals and other decision-makers must match government effort on the minimum ratio of one to one.

To be more specific: when Government invests in social over-head—education, cultural services, health, etc.—the citizens must match it by deploying at least an equivalent amount of their enthusiasm, talent, time, participation, drive, and utilisation. Or when Government invests in roads, natural resources, power and energy, transport systems, applied research, communications, price and non-price incentives, land development, water resources, and marketing facilities, to mention only a few, decision-makers at all levels must respond promptly. Where they originally produced for subsistence, they should now show a surplus output for sale; where they originally produced for the market, they must show a substantial net increase in output. Social and economic overhead is investment for deploying and expanding external economies; to get the maximum value out of it depends, to a large measure, upon full employment or maximum utilisation. Once government effort is matched and emulated by the millions of decision-makers throughout the economy, sustained economic and social progress is assured.

However, the rôle of Government is by no means limited to protecting voluntary areas of activity, or to laying down a proper infrastructure, or to providing opportunity of access. Government must directly or indirectly seek to achieve a more equitable distribution of economic power in order to supplement the efforts of the smaller decision-makers. Economic power means power to purchase as well as power to produce and sell. The two are only theoretically separate operations, sellers are also buyers and vice versa; also both forms of economic power have a money value and a real value. By real value is implied the amount of goods or services which a given quantum of money can fetch at current market values.

Clearly, the ups and downs of economic values have a bearing on economic power and therefore on its distribution. The rôle of government in this particular area is to ensure that real rather than money values are maintained. Attempts can be made to achieve this through a wages and incomes policy—a formal or informal regulation of wages, profits, interests, rents and prices in order to keep them in line with general productivity. Monetary policy may also be invoked through credit restriction, credit rationing, etc.; the growth in money supply can then keep pace with real economic growth. Fiscal policy too can play its part; the more traditional measures, taxation policy, planned expenditure programmes, rural credit, social security schemes, direct participation in production (agriculture, industry or tertiary services), and employment multiplier measures, can be employed. These growth, employment, and administrative measures, plus price stability measures, must be designed for achieving an increasingly more equitable distribution of real Kwacha votes and therefore general human welfare. It is, however, important to point out that in a man-centred society the decision-maker is not an adjunct to government or its structures, or its institutions, or its activities. He must regard such public measures as primarily an incentive for eliciting greater productivity in order to raise the quality of the human condition residence or citizenship.

CONCLUDING REMARKS

A mere introduction to the study of man and wealth needs no conclusion. In a book entitled *On the Road*, two beatniks speak out their minds. One says to the other:

Why, Sal, do you realise the shelves they build these days crack under the weight of knick-knack after six months or generally collapse? Same with houses, same with clothes. These bastards have invented plastics by which they could make houses that last for ever. And tyres! [people] are killing themselves by the millions every year with defective rubber tyres that get hot on the road and blow up. They could make tyres that never blow up. Same with tooth powder. There's a certain gum they've invented and they won't show it to anybody that if you chew it as a kid you'll never get a cavity for the rest of your born days. Same with clothes. They can make clothes that last for ever. They prefer making cheap goods so's everybody'll have to go on working and punching timeclocks and organising themselves in sullen unions and floundering around while the big grab goes on in Washington and Moscow.[2]

Whatever may be the images and realities of this observation from the beat generation, they echo our belief in man too. We have therefore suggested that humanism is life; it is the opposite of death. A dead decision-maker is one who has failed or ceased to see or develop to the full his social and economic capacities. He may continue to eat and sleep; he may even live more comfortably materially. Yet, to all intents and purposes, his *modus operandi* lacks intensity; it is guided by temporary values, and makeshift considerations. Indeed, it is not true that man was born free, it is also not true that he is automatically at the centre of society. In order to get to the centre, or in order to increase his measure of freedom, or in order to be alive, he has to engage in a ceaseless but productive life struggle. Only with such intensity of human purpose can the individual or human society sustain the balance between the spiritual and the material.

In any practical situation ends also derive significance from the existence and effectiveness of the means. Hence, it has been suggested that money is indispensable in our world: that there is no necessity for imagining an inherent conflict between money and humanism. Finally, humanism may not suggest any precise rules of thumb for socially acceptable economic behaviour. This would be a herculean task. But the considerations, the realities of the human condition, and the hopes which inspire it can do something. They can place economic behaviour in its proper context—the human context. They can, as it were, point out the richness, the inventiveness, and the creativeness, underlying and inspiring economic behaviour. By so doing they hope to open more windows and permit more light. And that also is the hope of this exercise.

2. J. Kerouac, *On the Road* (André Deutsch Ltd., N. York, 1968), p. 156.

5

HUMANISM AND THE ZAMBIAN ECONOMIC ORDER

Bastiaan de Gaay Fortman*

"In economic terms," President Kaunda has said, "Humanism is Socialism." Yet no economist would deny that the Zambian economy is still principally a capitalist economy. Thus there seems to be a problem of economic order in Zambia.

First of all we should clarify what is meant by terms like "capitalism" and "socialism". African leaders usually define these in a way quite different from that of economists. As Friedland and Rosberg have pointed out, African socialists tend to describe economic systems not in such formal terms as ownership of the means of production, but in terms of the human relationships to which these systems lead: "Capitalism is defined not simply as private ownership of the economy but as the kind of human relationships that individual ownership can produce."

Thus, President Nyerere has described capitalists as "loiterers", "parasites" and "exploiters of their fellow human beings". And Father Bede Onuoha has been even more outspoken in his contempt for capitalism: "Capitalism was responsible for the slave trade, colonialism and the wars. It has no respect for human dignity and has a long record of degrading exploitation of women, children and working men. Capitalism has no concern for unemployment. In one word, capitalism is the unleashing of human greed: it is *radically* wrong because it is based on a systematic selfishness and rugged individualism."

To African socialists capitalism means the organised exploitation of man by man. It destroys the high value placed on man in

---

*DR. BASTIAAN DE GAAY FORTMAN (Editor), Lecturer in Economics at the University of Zambia, "non-active" Fellow of the Free University, Amsterdam. Editor of a book on political renewal in the Netherlands (1967) and author of *Theory of Competition Policy* (1966) and many articles and essays on economic order and economic policy including *Het verval van de Schraperige Maatschappij* (The Decline of the Acquisitive Society).

traditional African societies. However, this does not imply that the
African socialist or Zambian humanist opts for a communist
economic system. Communism, too, is judged in terms of the human
relationships it produces. In a communist society, ideology is not
the servant of man but his master. There, society does not exist
for man but man for society. Like capitalism, such a system would
result in *alienation*. There is respect, for example, for China's
achievements but not for the Chinese communist methods. President
Kaunda puts it this way:

"The challenge of the time is how can we make mass development
in Zambia possible? Taking China as a lesson for us here—in
eighteen years they have managed to raise the standard of living
for all their people. Although we are a humanist and not a communist society we should nevertheless ask ourselves this question:
Can't we achieve the same, while retaining our humanism in
Zambia?"

When Dr. Kaunda identifies humanism with socialism, he is
thinking about socialism's concern to improve the quality of
people's lives: "one cardinal point in socialist thinking is the quality
of man". In the tribal community man was highly valued and there
was no exploitation of man by man in the sense in which such
exploitation is made possible by the acquisitive society whose
"whole tendency and interest and preoccupation is to promote
the acquisition of wealth" (Tawney). Humanism is a commitment
to improving the quality of people's lives in the face of an invading
money economy. On the one hand, specialisation and the use of
money can lead to a higher level of production, and Zambia
certainly needs more goods. On the other hand, money may result
in a reduction of all values to money values. And "specialisation
in its wake challenges very seriously a mutual aid society because
it could introduce selfishness and individualism of the Western
type of capitalism and could be very misleading". (Dr. Kaunda).

How is Zambia going to retain its high respect for man and
combat, or rather prevent, exploitation? What kind of economic
order will be created? It should be noted that Zambia inherited two
kinds of economic order. Firstly, there are the institutions and
organisation of a subsistence economy. While this economic system
is highly appreciated for its promotion of good human relationships some of its institutions may stand in the way of *development*.
The problem therefore is how to enable people to improve their

standard of living without breaking up their mutual aid society. Secondly, Zambia has inherited from Northern Rhodesia a money economy built on the principles of free enterprise, private ownership of resources and the profit motive. The development of this money economy was completely unrelated to the development of the people in the subsistence economy. It was there to serve the interests of white immigrants who had their roots not in the Zambian subsistence economy but in the developed money economies of Britain and South Africa. In economic books and articles Zambia is therefore always described as a "dual economy".

For people in the rural areas who wanted to advance themselves economically, there was no inducement whatsoever to stay in these areas and they consequently moved to the Copperbelt or some other area near the line of rail. In fact more people have moved than the money economy could absorb so that many have to live a subsistence life in the midst of the money economy. Therefore, development of the rural areas should be regarded not only as an end in itself but also as a means of preventing "poverty in the midst of plenty" in the money economy.

Today Zambia faces three main problems: (1) How to *Zambianise* its money economy. This is not merely a matter of replacing expatriates by Zambians but rather is it a problem of how to change the Western-orientated kind of society which the money economy tended to produce into a truly indigenous society. (2) The second main problem is how to make the money economy serve the development of the rural areas. (3) The third problem concerns the development of the present subsistence economy. This last problem which involves the achievement of a fuller life for *all* Zambians seems to be the most important one. It is this problem of *development* that dominated the President's speeches on "Humanism in Zambia". In his Mulungushi speech "Zambia towards economic Independence", President Kaunda formulated Zambian policies in relation to the problems of the already existing money economy. In this essay I shall first deal with the policies regarding the money economy and then briefly discuss Zambia's development policy.

A mixed economy

Zambia, as we have seen, rejects both the capitalist and the communist economic systems because of the kind of human relationships these systems produce. It does not want to copy any of the

Western economic systems. It wants to shape its own institutional framework for deciding the basic economic question of "What is to be produced, by what means and for whom?". The economic order can be defined as the way in which a society has distributed the power to decide on the production, distribution and consumption of goods and services. Capitalism places this power in the hands of the individual. The individual consumer decides what is to be produced, the individual producer decides how it will be done and the fruits of production go to the individual owners of resources. Co-ordination of the numerous economic decisions is effected through a system of markets and prices. In communism, on the other hand, economic power rests with the State which decides what is going to be produced and regulates the distribution of income. Co-ordination is done by planning.

This is not the place to discuss the merits and defects of the two economic systems. Suffice it to note that Zambia is well aware that in their pure forms capitalism and communism exist only in theory and that in practice the two economic systems are converging. In traditionally capitalist economies the rôle of the State in economic affairs is rapidly increasing while planning becomes more and more important; in the communist countries economic decision-making is being decentralised, profit incentives are being built into the system and the co-ordinating function of a price mechanism is increasingly recognised.

In the Zambian economy, too, both the individual and the State will play their part. Zambia will have a mixed economy. "A mixed economy," President Kaunda has said, "obviously means that we will borrow some of the good things—as well as some of the bad things, I am afraid—from either the capitalist or communist systems." Of course the aim is to borrow more good things than bad things.

Ideologically Zambia is unbiased. "We refuse to be dogmatic about anything," the President said in Mulungushi. Zambia does not hold the opinion that free enterprise on public ownership, for example, are either good or bad in themselves. The main criteria are human relationships and development: how does a particular institution serve man's development and the relationship between man and man. Africans have succeeded in creating a society in which man respects his fellow human beings and they wish to preserve their good human relationships. President Kaunda puts it this way: "Let the West have its Technology and Asia its Mysticism! Africa's gift to world culture must be in the realm of human relationships." If Africa tries to follow Western technological advancement without qualification, it may lose its own possession: good human relationships.

Thus, one may regard humanism as "Pragmatism" inspired by a striving for development and good human relationships. Let us now see what economic ideas Zambia has borrowed so far and what its own policies are.

Controlled private enterprise

Zambia, as we have seen, has inherited from Northern Rhodesia a free-enterprise economy. It still believes that free enterprise could work. "The very fact that we have declared ourselves in favour of a mixed economy is more than an indication that there is a place for individual initiative . . .", the President stated in Mulungushi. The problem is the *control* of free enterprise.

In the capitalist economic model, freedom of production is supposed to be controlled by freedom of consumption and *competition*. But in Zambia competition is lacking. There are great bottlenecks in supply and whoever manages to get the materials and goods despite the transport difficulties can sell them at very profitable prices. Today the money Zambia gets for its copper no longer goes to the Southern Rhodesia settler economy but is used for the development of Zambia's long-neglected infrastructure. This has created a great boom in nearly every type of economic activity. As a result, free enterprise in Zambia is far from a *self-controlling* institution. In his Mulungushi speech, President Kaunda announced certain measures and formulated certain rules which could control business.

Zambianisation

"We cannot declare ourselves in favour of private enterprise," the President said, "and forbid Zambians from participating in the private sector." The type of Zambianisation Mulungushi wishes to promote has to do with *managerial* rather than *technical* functions. Zambianisation of the technical functions can easily be left to private enterprise itself since this type of Zambianisation is in its own economic interest. There is little reason for complaint about the present pace of Zambianisation of technical functions, but there are still hardly any Zambian entrepreneurs: "The banks, the insurance companies, the building societies, the hire purchase companies and the other commercial financial institutions have not been very willing to assist the Zambian businessman." In order to stimulate the rise of Zambian entrepreneurs a number of measures have been taken such as limitation of local borrowing possibilities for resident expatriate enterprise in the hope that the banks and financial institutions will use their resultant excess liquidity for assisting Zambian business; exclusion of resident expatriate unspecialised business from the rural and "second class" trading areas; granting of road services licences and building minerals extracting permits to Zambian companies only; and the awarding of small contracts by the Public Works Department, and preferably also by the large private companies, only to Zambian businessmen.

There are, of course, good political reasons for Zambianisation of the economy. " . . . Time is now that we must take urgent and vigorous steps to put Zambian business firmly in the hands of the people themselves just as political power is in their hands," President Kaunda said. But there are also good economic reasons for managerial Zambianisation. Zambia was, as the President put it, being exploited as a nation by foreign capitalists. In this respect he remarked: "It is difficult to stop such exploitation without first of all involving Zambians themselves." Net profit rates of 30 per cent with gross profit rates of 70 per cent and more are the rule in Zambia rather than the exception. Foreign capitalists used to borrow a certain amount of money locally which they multiplied by doing business and then exported. *Zambian* businessmen on the other hand can be expected to reinvest their money locally.

Thus, Zambianisation of entrepreneurs could be a means of preventing the exploitation of Zambia *as a nation*. But, some people might say, black Zambians are not necessarily better people than white expatriates. Zambianisation would offer little guarantee against exploitation of man by man in Zambia. It should be remarked here that President Kaunda is no less against exploitation of Zambians by Zambians than he is opposed to exploitation of *Zambia* by expatriates: "It is important to remember that as humanists we cannot allow Zambians to develop into capitalists at all and here is where a serious problem arises. In the final analysis all this boils down to one major point. Our society through its institutions—its man-made institutions—must fight with all it has at its disposal against the exploitation of man by man in whatever field."

Zambia wants *controllable* free enterprise, that is private enterprise to which the public interest can be communicated. This is the basic message of Mulungushi. It will be easier for the Government to communicate its ideas to Zambian businessmen than to expatriates. Zambian entrepreneurs have no alternative but to do business *in Zambia*. They are also likely to be more conscious of the political climate and ethical views prevailing in Zambia.

Fair distribution of income and wealth

The objective, as we saw, is Zambianisation of society, and not just substitution of rich Zambians for rich expatriates. President Kaunda is well aware of the dangers of creating a Zambian entrepreneurial class:

"Let it be emphasised, however, that the more we interest our people in this particular field the more they will be exposed to dangers I have referred to already—those of becoming a money-centred society. Wealth, like knowledge or an other instrument of service to man we can think of, becomes an instrument of oppression and suppression if we do not handle it properly. Very often we discuss the problem of distributing wealth equally among our people. There are many reasons why this is important. Major among these, however, are that we want each one of our four million people to live a fuller life and, secondly, wealth that is concentrated in the hands of a few people is a danger to any society in that those in whose hands wealth was centred would become exploiters of their fellow men in more than one way and this is no good both for those whom they exploit as well as for themselves."

In order to prevent Zambian "business barons" from emerging, President Kaunda has announced that Zambian enterprises when they reach a certain size may be invited to sell a controlling interest to the State. Mwaiseni Stores Ltd. with equity capital of K150,000 and a turnover in 1967 of K1,500,000 has already been invited to do this. This size may be an indication of the approximate dividing line between private and State-controlled enterprise in trading in Zambia.

It seems that the problems connected with Zambianisation of the money economy will be not so much in the sphere of *control* of the economy but in the sphere of *distribution* of income and wealth. The differences which in Northern Rhodesia used to be differences between Whites, Asians and Africans are now becoming differences between Zambians and Zambians. This was no doubt inevitable. Government could not at once pull down all the attractive houses in the so-called "low density areas" nor could it afford to build this type of house for the people in the "high density areas". Neither would it be possible to convince Zambian civil servants that they should work on salaries considerably lower than those of their expatriate colleagues. It may be regretted that Zambia inherited these colonial inequalities; it seems doubtful, however, whether Government could have prevented this. What it *could do* now is to prevent a further increase of inequality.

First and foremost Zambia should create and preserve equality of *opportunity*. If good education, for instance, has to be financed by private means, inequality will be passed down from generation to generation. Differences in income and wealth can be modified by ensuring equality of opportunity.

At present a factor that may retard the forming of *classes* based on income and wealth is the *extended family system*. Poor people tend to remind their more fortunate relatives of the general pattern of poverty in the country. Some indication that the African might be more sensitive towards the importance of community in life lies in the fact that, however great a nuisance people might consider their poor relatives, they will very rarely break with their family. Provided *nepotism* is fought against, the extended family system might continue to work as a force against class formation. It is President Kaunda's hope that through the extended family system Zambia will remain an *accepting* and *inclusive* society. Thus, the creation of a Western type of Welfare State—where Government guarantees a minimum amount of welfare to all its citizens because private initiative would surely fail to take care of the less fortunate—might not become necessary.

There are several good reasons why an attempt should be made to stop the *rural exodus*. One reason is that it breaks up families and communities and may lead to a vacuum of values for the new town immigrants. Another reason is that it aggravates inequality. Even if Government can succeed in reducing inequality among those who work in wage employment, it will never be able to provide jobs and housing for *everybody* if people should continue to move in such great numbers from the rural areas to the towns.

At present there are many who are forced to live a subsistence life in the midst of a flourishing money economy. This is not a very healthy situation.

Stopping the rural exodus means developing the rural areas and providing equal opportunities for the people living there. For this purpose the Government needs money and above all the commitment of the people working in the present money economy. Time and again, President Kaunda and his ministers try to explain to workers that high wage demands and strikes amount to "workers exploiting peasants". In Mulungushi the President remarked: "Today there is so much talk but very little action of developed countries helping developing ones. We must fight this within our own country."

In a developing country such as Zambia, labour has to be effectively controlled. However, control can be effective only if it is also just. Therefore high incomes have to be controlled and excessive spending or profiteering by high income earners—on houses for example—must be discouraged. Unlike Arusha, Mulungushi failed to deal with the high income earners. Because it may be difficult to change the colonial-inherited wages and salaries structure, as a first step towards greater equality the colonial-inherited taxation structure might be revised.

Nationalisation ?

Should we conclude from the Mulungushi takeovers that Zambia is basically biased towards public enterprise? In my opinion this would be the wrong conclusion. The principal reason for the takeovers was that Government did not want the fruits of its self-created boom to be taken entirely by foreign and expatriate enterprise, to be consumed or reinvested outside Zambia. This point is emphasised in the "Background" preceding the official publication of the President's economic policy speech: "Instead of the expatriate enterprises accepting their profits and at the same time ploughing as much as possible into the development and redevelopment of their business, it became evident that they were obsessed with 'making hay while the sum shines' and expatriated increasingly large portions of their profits." On the President's invitation to 25 enterprises to give the State a 51 per cent controlling interest the "Background" comments: "The measures announced in His Excellency's Speech, although they involve in many cases assuming controlling interest in some enterprises, fall far short of nationalisation as conventionally known."

There is a remarkable difference between Tanzania's *Arusha Declaration* and Zambia's *Mulungushi Declaration*. In Arusha President Nyerere declared: "The way to build and maintain socialism is to ensure that the major means of production are under the control and ownership of the Peasants and Workers themselves through their Government and their co-operatives." Next, the *major means of production* were specified and nationalisation announced of those not yet under the control and ownership of the people's Government. The firms whose ownership was affected were not many but they were *key enterprises*. The list was small, President Nyerere said, "because, in the words of Norman Mailer, 'You can't nationalise nothing'." Basically, Tanzania does not believe in private enterprise.

Zambia, on the other hand, believes in *controlled private enterprise*. The Government has taken a controlling interest in 25 companies which in no way could be described as *key enterprises*. At the same time it has amended its exchange control regulations to allow foreign-controlled companies—including the two big mining companies—to remit dividends abroad only in so far as those dividends do not exceed 30 per cent of their equity capital nor 50 per cent of their profits. The two measures are interrelated. Government wants private business to *develop* the Zambian economy —allowance being made for fair profits—but not to *exploit* it. The 51 per cent takeovers might be regarded as *controlling measures*: Government is now able to influence these enterprises. If the aim were not to control but to run the firms in question, the Government would have fully nationalised them.

Mulungushi, as I understand it, wants to *communicate a certain message to private enterprise in Zambia:* the country would like to see it making reasonable but not excessive profits, and it would like it to adopt a *Zambian* investment policy. The Government does not want to nationalise all the key enterprises such as the mining companies and the banks. (Unlike the Tanzanian banks, the Zambian Banks do not export more capital than they import.) These companies are now supposed to play the game. The banks could defy Government policy for some time by not lending at all—not to expatriates because that has been made difficult by the Mulungushi measures, and not to Zambians because they do not like the Mulungushi measures. And the mining companies, too, could frustrate Government by letting unexported profits accumulate instead of using them for extended prospecting and development, or for alternative investments. (More intensive mining development also demands a change of the royalty formula which is at present on output instead of profits. Such a change was indeed announced in Mulungushi.) If they chose to ignore Government intentions, these enterprises, too, might be invited to sell a 51 per cent interest in their shares to Government. But this measure would not then be taken *con amore* but because private enterprise did not wish to play the game.

The 25 companies in which Government has now a 51 per cent interest were selected for two main reasons. Firstly, they all made their profits on the domestic market; some of them were actually profiteering. By taking a controlling interest in these, Government will be better equipped to protect the Zambian consumer than it was through its price control agency. If these firms continue to make big profits, the public will benefit from this through the State.

Some of the firms in question could serve Zambia's *industrial development policy* much better than they did. "So far," President Kaunda said, "we have tried to promote State Enterprise the hard way. We have confined our new business activities through the Industrial Development Corporation to certain special types of enterprises, which have generally been the hardest to develop." Apparently, it was Government's feeling that industrial development could be speeded up by taking over certain enterprises which operated in the same field as the Government's Industrial Development Corporation (INDECO) in order to control and co-ordinate these firms' *investment policies*.

Negotiations over the sale of shares to the State—especially in the case of the companies taken over to help the Government's industrial development policy—have been generally satisfactory and to the approval of both parties. Although sale of shares means a loss of potential profits, it also may imply more security in business. Firms for which profit expectations and the risk of loss (including the risk of full nationalisation) are fairly balanced, may actually welcome State participation. If they operate in the same field as INDECO or in related fields, they may be invited to sell a controlling interest at some time in the future. Market controlling firms which are sure to continue to make large profits—such as the breweries now taken over—might be less pleased with enforced State participation. Market controlling firms not yet taken over may now be deterred from setting exorbitant prices and not reinvesting their profits.

The main importance of the takeovers is to show private enterprise in general that Government will not shrink from taking a 51 per cent interest in companies if this appears to be the best way of controlling them. Thus the emphasis in Mulungushi was on *controlling* rather than on *running* private enterprise. Government's ideas are well illustrated by President Kaunda's remarks on Government's relationship with the mining companies: "We don't have the ability to run mines on our own; we have the ability to tax the mines. For participation in the mines our idea is to get some more shares."

So much for the interpretation of President Kaunda's economic policy speech. The next question is: What should we think of this policy? First of all, it is a *consistent* policy. (Only if the Mulungushi measures are regarded as a move towards *controlled private enterprise* do they show consistency; if they are seen as a move towards full nationalisation how then to explain the relative unimportance of the companies taken over?) It is a pragmatic policy with a clearly recognisable pattern: Government does not want to run business, but wants to promote reinvestment of excess profits and it wants to increase gradually the potential and influence of its own Industrial Development Corporation. It will take a controlling interest in firms if this is necessary in order to secure control or to speed up development.

Could Zambia's pragmatic policy of controlled private enterprise work? There are two sides to this question. Firstly, is it a good policy from the point of view of the country's development? Secondly, will private enterprise accept it? Let us take the latter question first.

Nowhere in the world would private enterprise like to fall into the hands of a bureaucracy. It abhors this probably more than relatively low profit expectations. Therefore a policy of controlled private enterprise is not easy. It requires that the rules are clearly formulated and that administrative decisions affecting business are taken quickly. After Mulungushi there was some confusion as to what certain measures exactly meant. This could have been avoided if it had been realised that business needs clear-cut rules rather than policy statements. The "common business-man", whether one likes it or not, has little feeling for, nor great interest in, politics; therefore it should have been carefully explained to him what Mulungushi meant for the running of his business.

It is, of course, impossible, to make unambiguous rules. Administration of law always contains an element of *law-finding*. This is especially so in the field of economic law, in which there is a continous confrontation with the dynamics of economic life. Hence administrators of economic law should be of the "managerial" rather than "civil service" type; they should be decision-makers. Fortunately, in the execution of Zambia's economic policy much responsibility is in the hands of the Industrial Development Corporation in which the managerial spirit prevails. Such measures as foreign exchange control and import licensing, too, should be carried out in a managerial rather than in a bureaucratic spirit. If the Government's managers understand the law and its intention and are known for their integrity, quick decision-making will bring nothing but advantages.

If Government is careful not to confront private enterprise with too much red tape and uncertainty and continue to allow reasonable profits, I see no reason why Zambia's policy of controlling rather than running economic life should fail because of resistance by private enterprises. But now the second question: is it a good policy for the development of the country? I think it is, mainly for two reasons.

Firstly, if Zambia's money economy is to serve the development of its subsistence economy it should produce a capital surplus rather than absorb the country's scarce capital. In Zambia's present stage of development it seems essential that for industrial investment decisions, unadjusted profitability is considered a *sine qua non*. In other words, it seems extremely dangerous to abandon the rule that private revenues should exceed private costs. If Government were to manage the country's whole industrial development alone, it might be tempted to engage in too many expensive projects—for example iron and steel plants, and other forms of heavy industry—simply because the advanced economies happen to have such industries. "Copy-development" would be dangerously tempting. Every project for which the norm of simple profitability has been abandoned is continuously *capital-absorbing*. Yet at this stage, the country's capital could, and in my opinion should, be carefully

husbanded to produce more *development* in the agricultural sphere—
if at least one understands by development opportunities for *all*
people to develop themselves. If it is agreed that in its *industrial
investment* Zambia should in general stick to the profitability norm
as an essential, private enterprise would be the best watchdog.
(I do not dispute that Government should adopt an industrial
development policy which selects projects not on the basis of
maximum profitability but with the help of criteria relating to
maximum *development*. But also for these projects it would be
dangerous to abandon the rule of unadjusted profitability as a
sine qua non. See also S. H. Goodman's contribution to this book.)

The second reason why I feel Zambia's policy of controlled private
enterprise is good for the country is that the problems of development in the rural areas demand the full attention of Government
and the ruling Party. To take full responsibility for the country's
industrial sector would at present be too large and unnecessary a
burden. I have already expressed the opinion that agricultural
development today is more important for Zambia than industrial
development. This is also the view of Zambian Humanism. It is
time now to discuss Humanism and development.

Humanism and economic development

"Humanism in Zambia is a decision in favour of rural areas";
" . . . the future of the country economically is on the land"; and
" . . . my main concern is in the village", these are some statements
by President Kaunda which clearly show the key importance
attached to development of the rural areas. These statements are
not self-evident; indeed some economists may disagree with the
President's preference for agricultural development. Their argument
might be: most underdeveloped economies try to grow by improving
agriculture. If Zambia does the same, the dangers of oversupply
on the world market for agricultural products will be increased.
Let Zambia, which already has the advantage of a copper-mining
industry, grow by industrial rather than by agricultural expansion.
The economists' argument seems quite convincing. But its defect
is that it is an *exclusively economic* argument. Economists are
primarily concerned with economic growth which is usually defined
as "growth of real national income *per capita*". Zambian Humanism on the other hand is primarily concerned with *development:*
opportunities for *all* people in Zambia to attain a fuller life. As

President Kaunda put it: "National development is meaningless if it does not develop each one of our four million people in the country". Whereas industrial expansion may be very important in terms of growth of national income, agricultural development will remain the main norm because that affects the development of the *people*. Besides, agricultural development will remain important for a long time to come even from the purely economic point of view because Zambia is far from self-sufficient in respect of quantity and quality of the food it needs.

President Kaunda has defined the objectives of the country not in terms of growth of national income but in terms of development:

"(*a*) No person should starve in Zambia because there is no real land hunger as is the case in many other parts of the world.

(*b*) No person should really fail to have a decent two- or three-roomed Kimberley brick house.

(*c*) No person should really ever dress in rags in Zambia nor indeed go barefooted.

(*d*) No person should really ever suffer from malnutrition in Zambia."

These objectives are not to be attained through maximum growth of national income and subsequent redistribution of this among the villagers but through development of the people themselves. The first National Development Plan formulated the aim of helping people to develop themselves as follows:

"To minimise the inherited economic imbalance between the urban and rural sectors with a view to raising the capacity of the latter sector for transforming resources into social and economic growth."

Development of the people in the rural areas demands the full commitment of the Government and the ruling Party: " . . . one of the principal tasks of the leaders must be to encourage 'development from below'. . . . What is required is to go to [the people] and encourage local initiative at the village level if it is in the rural areas, and at the section level if it is in the urban areas. . . . To encourage local initiative it is important that the first question our people should ask is '*What is it that we can do to develop ourselves in various fields and where and when is government help required?*'"

It has already been realized by Zambian leaders that a mistake was made by introducing too many tractors in the rural areas. A tractor is a highly capital-intensive piece of equipment which can replace more than a hundred people working with hoes. To introduce tractors now, means thinking in terms of economic growth instead of development. People might tend to see the tractor not so much as a means of increasing productivity but as a means of increasing leisure. They do not view such equipment in relation to the development of themselves. From the point of view of development it might be much better to try to convince the people that they should procure oxen ploughs. In this regard the President remarked in Mulungushi:

"If we equate development and progress only with the number of tractors used, with the number of big projects, with a small number of well-looking areas, and with the town only, then we will soon face very big problems: we will not be able to avoid greater unemployment at the end of a year and, much more so, at the end of our Four Year Development Plan. Development that is restricted to only a small part of the economic sector, to only a few regions, to only large-scale production, and to only highly capital-intensive techniques is, in my view, no development at all.

"These described and often prevailing facts in many countries make it absolutely necessary to follow a different orientation of economic planning. Economic planning must learn to see the virtues of real development, of small industrialisation; it must realise the potential in utilising human beings where they are and in reaching a self-sustained growth in all regions and sectors of the economy."

It would of course go far beyond the scope of the present article to deal with all the possibilities and difficulties of Zambia's development policy. Dr. Elliott in his contribution to this book discusses the Zambian "agrarian revolution" in detail. It was our aim here merely to explain that Humanism with its concern for the quality of people's lives means a commitment towards *development* as opposed to the narrower notion of economic growth.

The co-operative approach

There is one more point which demands our attention because of its importance for the Zambian economic order: the idea of co-operative enterprise. Co-operatives are regarded as the basis of economic development in Zambia, particularly in the rural areas. Production co-operatives already existed in Zambia before Independence. But since 1964 many new co-operatives have been formed, mainly in the spheres of building and farming. There are two main reasons why the co-operative is considered to be the ideal form of enterprise.

In the first place, a co-operative is the institutional embodiment of *co-operation* among people: "We are, in fact, basing all our activities on a mutual aid society, on a co-operative approach of life. [Humanism] is a philosophy of joint service by individuals in a community." (Dr. Kaunda.) We have already observed that the mutual aid society is not seen as an innovation in Zambia, but is based on the traditional village unit.

In the second place, co-operatives are regarded as a means of promoting economic democracy. President Kaunda explained this idea as follows: "I look at these co-operatives as another way of establishing democracy. People will begin to debate things publicly, first of all at village level, ward level, district level and then national level. Co-operatives are a very good beginning for this sort of thing."

In practice, the co-operative movement in Zambia is still by no means an unqualified success. One problem is lack of *management* and *authority*. Democracy does not require *lack* of authority but *control* of authority by those over whom it is exercised. The authority of the Chairman and the Secretary of a co-operative is not very great, perhaps because their authority is not functional in the sense that they are the people who unmistakably know most about farming and marketing agricultural products.

Another problem co-operatives sometimes face is lack of unity and common purpose. Internal quarrels not seldom occur, particularly in the collectively worked co-operative farms. This is perhaps not surprising in a group in which the individual's income is dependent on the work of all and where those who work hard might not reap the full benefits of their labour because of the laziness of others.

An even more serious problem arises when members confine the co-operative spirit to their internal relations but see no objection in exploiting other people. It has not been unusual to borrow money from the Government to set up a co-operative and then to use these public funds to employ other people as workmen.

The President does not feel happy about this. He once described it as "becoming small capitalists on public funds".

Should these problems lead to the conclusion that the co-operative movement in Zambia is doomed to fail? This would be an unfortunate conclusion which would imply giving up the whole Humanist approach. President Kaunda has formulated the relationship between Humanism and the co-operative movement in very strong terms: "A co-operative approach is a way of life, and it is true to say that the whole Humanist approach is a co-operative one, it is based on co-operatives." I do not think the problems of co-operatives in practice will doom the whole co-operative approach to failure although these problems may render necessary some rethinking on its implementation.

The aim in Zambia is to build a co-operative movement on the traditional mutual aid society. Therefore its basic unit should be the village or group of villages rather than an artificially formed group of about twenty people. The importance of the village has been greatly emphasised by the President: "Our ability to maintain and develop the traditional community based on mutual aid society principles demand that we recognise the village or section as the most important political, economic, social, scientific and cultural unit for development." Co-operation in the village is more natural and more effective than in the idealistic form of co-operative enterprise. The latter consists of a group of people who, having nothing in common but their ideals, come together to share everything, both work and income. It has also been tried in the West where it arose from the ideas of utopian socialists as an understandable reaction to the lack of community in economic life inherent in nineteenth century capitalism. It has not met with much success, perhaps because the kind of co-operative it wanted to establish was not rooted in any natural community and perhaps because it underestimated man's desire for some sort of independence.

The more successful production co-operatives in Europe were formed because of economic necessity. Small farmers or market gardeners, for example, could get access to the economies of scale enjoyed by their large competitors only by starting co-operation. In their co-operatives, individual farming remained of primary importance. In Zambia, too, we find "individual farms organised on co-operative lines", the so-called service co-operatives. These existed already before Independence, particularly in the Eastern

Province. If co-operatives should not be incidental groups of idealists but a *general movement*, it may be wise to encourage service co-operatives in particular. Such co-operatives may turn out to be the most *stable* ones because they are based on economic advantage and rooted in traditional Zambian forms of co-operation. Government should be careful not to create too many *artificial* incentives for *collective* co-operatives.

Co-operation in the traditional village concerns only those activities in which people cannot help themselves. A defect of the idealistic form of co-operative, in which total income is equally shared by all members, is that it also helps people who could very well help themselves but who are too lazy to do so. Of course, the co-operative can expel its lazy members but their behaviour may already have created unnecessary tensions. In the village the individual farmer works on his own plot and the fruits of his labour are primarily for himself and the people with whom he is living together. There is personal responsibility: the responsibility of each individual person for himself and his immediate family. From the humanist point of view there seems to be nothing wrong with individual responsibilities as long as *communal* responsibilities are not neglected. And indeed in the traditional village they are not. People help each other in production—when certain activities demand co-operation—and in consumption—through the extended family system.

It might be a good idea to build the co-operative movement in Zambia upon the traditional co-operation in the villages and to consider the villages as the basic co-operative units. The problem of lack of management could perhaps be overcome by setting up a service organisation shared by all farmers of the village and run by a trained and experienced farm manager. To make the service units economically viable, some village regrouping might be attempted— through persuasion rather than coercion.

The present plan to form co-operative unions which will provide the various co-operatives in an area with technical equipment and managerial advice seems a good one. The unions will serve also the individual farmers in the area. Collective co-operatives would not have to be abolished but a certain amount of private responsibility for private plots might be encouraged to prevent unnecessary tensions. The union plan can take the villages as basic units of development; it seems in line with the kind of co-operation existing in the traditional villages.

In countries where the spirit of community has faded away and where landlordism prevails, it may be necessary to abolish private farming completely and enforce some sort of collectivisation upon people. But in Zambia it might not be wise to do away with the private farmer. Certainly, in the transition from subsistence agri-culture to commercial farming there is a danger of abuses and loss of the communal spirit. To prevent capitalist forms of wage-employ-ment, whether by individual farmers or by collective co-operatives, rules could perhaps be made, demanding that where there is co-operation in work, there should also be profit-sharing. Although *collectivisation* could perhaps be enforced upon people, with *co-operation* this will not be possible. Government should limit itself to creating the organisational framework and the rules within which the farmers might find their own ways of co-operation.

*   *   *

Zambia is attempting to retain a society with good human relation-ships in its process of economic development and change. For this purpose the nation has been equipped with the philosophy of Humanism and the connected policies of controlled private enter-prise, development from below, and economic co-operation. Everything will depend now upon the response from the people, both Zambians and expatriates, and on Government's and the ruling Party's faithfulness to their self-proclaimed ideals.

6

HUMANISM AND THE AGRICULTURAL REVOLUTION

Dr Charles Elliott*

In almost every country in Africa the development of agriculture
has come to occupy a central place in the political philosophy of
the ruling party. In Kenya political revolution was born of land
hunger. In Tanzania *Ujamaa* is above all else a policy for the
villages. In the Congo one of the focal points of political debate
has been the carving up of the former European land holdings. If
Zambia is very different from these countries economically, politically the same basic situation pertains, namely that the vast bulk of
the electorate, in Zambia's case some 85 per cent, live in the villages.
Any political formulation or creed is therefore bound to reflect
the aspirations and needs of this rural population. Like *Ujamaa*,
Zambian Humanism is not merely a policy document nor a search
for an abstract political philosophy. It is perhaps both these things
and yet many more. Giving them a limited cohesion is a concern
not so much for the standard of living as the quality of life. This
fundamental distinction must be grasped. The standard of living is
only one component of the quality of life. The others are human
relations, economic organisation, the distribution of political power,
the manner of the exercise of authority and the total physical,
moral and spiritual environment in which life is lived. In its current
embryonic state, the philosophy of humanism seeks to offer broad
perspectives within which detailed policy formulations can be
worked out on all these components of the quality of life. It is
therefore mistaken to search for a detailed series of policies on
any one topic and to assess them against the actual situation.

*DR. CHARLES ELLIOTT is Reader in Economics at the University of Zambia,
and an Anglican Priest. He has a small farm near Lusaka. Before coming to
Zambia in 1965 Dr. Elliott worked at the United Nations Research Institute
for Social Development in Geneva on problems of agricultural development.
His writings include a study of land concentration and economic growth,
Tenure systems and constraints on agricultural change, and *The ideology of
economic growth*.

Although it is true that actual policies—even in very great detail—are sometimes offered, in general Zambian Humanism offers more of a series of guidelines to practical political thinking than a code of well-defined political means to accurately pinpointed ends.

Precisely because it is the political equivalent, as it were, of a proximate ethic, Zambian Humanism is notoriously difficult to relate to identifiable policies. There is so often a policy gap between broad aims of an improvement in the quality of life and the world of hard reality. This is inevitable and, at this stage, admirable, since it opens the way for public debate not only on the ends but also on the means. As we shall argue later in this essay, this may be one of the most important contributions that the whole humanism debate can make, not only to the quality of political life in Zambia, but also to agricultural development.

What follows can be divided into four parts. First we shall discuss the basic ideas on agricultural development, contained in the published works on humanism, and especially in President Kaunda's speech at Mulungushi in April 1968. Next we shall identify some of the fundamental problems in Zambian agriculture. In the third section we will explore the extent to which the President's published writings and his speeches relate to the fundamental problems. Lastly, we shall turn to the policy gap and suggest ways in which the basic ideas of humanism can be incorporated into practical policies that will achieve the philosophical ends of humanism by means consistent with it.

Agriculture and Humanism

The implications of humanism for agriculture can be broadly divided into production policies, and policies for farm organisation.

As far as production is concerned there are two considerations. The first is Zambia's continuing reliance upon imported foodstuffs. Although the President mentions this in his writings, his most outspoken comments came in his Mulungushi speech. He gave a detailed list of products that Zambia was then importing, together with the annual value of imports that could be produced at home. Concern with import substitution, however, does not centre on the foreign balance. The point is more fundamental still. Every imported good implies a loss of income to Zambians. Food imports of over K20 million in 1966 therefore imply a loss of that order of magnitude to the Zambian farming sector.[1] This represents about one-third of the total sales of the whole agricultural sector in 1966.

The second basic consideration in production policies is the President's evident concern for standards of nutrition and the standard of living of the rural population. As is well known, it was largely the President's personal initiative that established the Food and Nutrition Commission in Zambia in 1967 and his personal concern that the level of protein intake should be increased throughout the country is therefore reflected in his thinking about production policies. It is perhaps important to emphasise that so far as can be detected from the published material, he regards improvements in nutrition as ends in themselves rather than necessary means to increased productivity. This is clearly a direct deduction from basic humanist principles. It differentiates the President's thinking from that of an increasing number of economists who regard social inputs such as improvements in nutrition as prerequisites of increased productivity. These two emphases are not of course mutually inconsistent: rather are they mutually reinforcing, for they both aim at breaking out of one of the many vicious circles that afflict traditional agriculture. In both the *Guide to the Implementation of Humanism* and his Mulungushi speech, the President gives a high priority to breaking the circle of poverty, ignorance and undernourishment. For instance, in the *Guide to the Implementation*, he seems to place upon it the very highest priority: "the first thing Zambia must do is to think of how to grow the right type of food for its nationals, and of course to show them how and when to use these." The *Guide to the Implementation* further contains a considerable lecture on the principles of nutrition and a classification of Zambian agricultural products according to their nutritional status. As we shall see later, this contains direct policy implications which, as is to be expected at this stage of the debate, are not fully worked out.

It is important to consider the extent to which the two ends of production policy are mutually consistent. Since the bulk of Zambia's food imports are meat, vegetables and fruit, it obviously follows that any attempt to replace these imports with home production will also simultaneously have the effect of widening the diet available to the rural population. It is precisely the obsession with maize,

---

1. Assuming that imported inputs would be small or negligible.

nutritionally an unsatisfactory crop, which has led to the functional inefficiency which, as we shall describe below, is reflected in the high level of imports of higher priced foodstuffs. Both ends of production policy therefore imply a diversification of agricultural production which is nothing new in Zambian agricultural thinking. But it also implies that this diversification affects all producers. In the past diversification has often been thought of in terms of large-scale enterprise, either private or state; Zambian humanism seems to imply diversification of production right down to the smallest village farmer. We shall argue below that this is a most significant shift in thinking.

If the implications for humanism are clear in relation to production policy, the same is not wholly true of policies for farm organisation. Again and again, in his writings and his speeches, the President insists that the traditional village society was a mutual aid society. The most obvious modern incarnation of this principle would appear to be the primary productive co-operative society. As we would expect, therefore, the President does indeed lay much emphasis on the development of primary societies in agriculture. In his address to the national council of U.N.I.P. on the 9th April 1965, and quoted in the *Guide to the Implementation of Humanism*, the President said: "If the co-operative movement in Zambia is meant to be a way of life and not just a way of solving our unemployment problems, then it is desirable that all of us should give it serious thought. In trying to philosophise on co-operative activities as they affect us, we should recall that from the cradle to the grave most Zambian people of old lived in the co-operative way. This had been accepted as a way of life without the philosophising of pundits and there is no earthly reason why we should not be proud of it, for it was enjoyed by our ancestors." After having given what some may regard as a rather idealised description of traditional village life, the President continued: "Quite honestly to me this is very appealing and the way of life I would like to see developed and adapted to suit the present age, in many ways a much more difficult time. The people of old obviously realised that unity is strength . . . but more than this our ancestors realised and appreciated the importance of the individual . . . We might now ask ourselves a very relevant question and this is: how do we now organise our society on the basis of the importance of the individual and how can we ensure that what the individual does is for the good of society as a whole?"

The President faces this question but it is at least doubtful whether he gives a complete answer from the point of view of farm organisation. On the one hand, he describes the benefits, economic, social and relational, which stem from co-operative enterprise; and on the other hand he realises that an appreciation of the significance of the individual lies very near to the heart of humanism. Translated into farm organisational terms, then, he is faced with a choice between organising the sector on a co-operative basis on the one hand, and on the other organising the sector as the ideal of the small peasant farmer enjoying, and judged by, the fruits of his own labour.

As far as the first alternative is concerned, the President is well aware of the difficulties and of the dismal history of co-operative endeavour in Africa as a whole. He also implies a recognition of the fact that the establishment of co-operatives does not necessarily lead to a co-operative spirit. As the Dumont report emphasised, exploitation of his fellows by one individual is made easier rather than more difficult within the framework of a co-operative organisation. Certainly the experience of the Zambian Government in establishing co-operatives has been somewhat unhappy. Launched with enthusiasm in 1964, the co-operative development programme was probably the least sucessful endeavour of the independent Government in the whole field of agriculture. By 1967 the lack of leadership and the lack of sufficiently close supervision of co-operatives then in existence brought the formation of new co-operatives almost to a halt. Given the critical shortage of trained agricultural manpower in the country, and the enormous distances involved in close supervision, it will be a long time before resources are adequate to develop successfully primary societies on the scale that is ambivalently implied in the President's documents.

But while there are practical objections to the wide-scale adoption of co-operative organisations, there are philosophical objections to the development of the agricultural sector by individual peasant farmers. Repeatedly the President inveighs against a western type of individualism and in his Mulungushi speech, for instance, he states quite categorically that there is no place in Zambia for individual capitalism. But a type of agricultural organisation which depends heavily upon individual peasant farmers is likely to throw up a number of individual capitalists. Originally, no doubt they would be capitalists on a very small scale but the more successful would eventually emerge as large-scale farmers, indistinguishable in their operations from European farmers. This would be entirely contrary to the whole spirit of Zambian Humanism. The President thus falls back on a rather vague concept of the village unit. Within the village unit the farm organisation may be co-operative or it may be individual. In either event the traditional values of mutual aid are to be maintained. The profit motive is to give place to the ideal of mutual service and the knowledge and skill of the individual is to be laid at the command of the community. The village production council is to ensure that correct production policies are followed and that the good of the community is put above the good of the individual.

Negatively, we may say that this looks like a reformulation of traditional society with the added garnish of a village production council. The political and economic dynamic seems to be lacking. After all, what kept the traditional village together was the fear of outside intruders and the necessity of self-preservation. With this dynamic removed, it is difficult to see what force is going to ensure the patterns of behaviour implied in this type of organisation. The obvious answer is the development of the country but, as we shall emphasise later, so far the Government has failed to project the demands of development as a categorical imperative.

Positively, it appeared from the Mulungushi speech that the President no longer subscribes to the view first and most forcibly expressed in the Seers Report, that the way to increase and diversify production is by the large-scale adoption of state production units. Although he mentions these in the *Guide to the Implementation of Humanism*, the evidence suggests that between writing the *Guide* and speaking at Mulungushi, his thought had grown to the realisation that the centrality of man and the rediscovery of traditional values do not easily coexist with massive state farms, which necessarily imply the perpetuation of employer/employee relationships. The majority of state farms which avoid these relationships, such as the notorious Chombwa Cotton Scheme, have not been noticeably successful. While it may be true that state production units accounted for only a small proportion of the Ministry of Agriculture's budget, they did, until 1968, play a leading rôle in that Ministry's development strategy. To this extent, then, the further elaboration of the principles of humanism may well prove to have had a significant effect on the development strategy in agriculture. If this is the case, it implies a fall in the rate of growth of output in the agricultural sector, a reduction in efficiency and a slowdown in the diversification of production. This could be particularly unfortunate in the case of beef production, since the output of weaners by the State ranches is an essential condition of rapidly increasing beef production. At this level there is, therefore, a conflict between import substitution on the one hand and the form of farm organisation implied by humanism on the other. A compromise will therefore have to be reached between principles and pragmatism. A likely outcome is that state ranches already established will continue as planned, but that the number of new state ranches and state production units will fall much below that originally envisaged.

So much then for the broad implications of humanism for the agricultural sector. We now turn to an examination of the principal problems in the sector.

Problems in Zambian agriculture

The most convenient way of examining the fundamental problems in Zambian agriculture is to consider the functions that the agricultural sector should perform in a developing country. Clearly, the primary task of the sector is to supply food to the nation as a whole. The subsistence sector, by definition, supplies food for itself and in a fully subsistence economy does not export food to the other sectors. As far as the subsistence sector is concerned, then, the primary object is to produce as wide a range of foods as the natural endowment permits, with the minimum of input on behalf of the subsistence cultivators. This end must be achieved without undermining the long-run fertility of the soil and without risk of famine. If famine is recurrent, or if the diet is inadequate, or if land is abused, then the sector may be said to be functionally inefficient. In the case of present-day Zambia, except under very unusual climatic conditions, actual famine is uncommon, though some of the so-called Cinderella provinces are net importers of maize. There are signs that this situation is changing, e.g. it is highl probable that the Northern Province will achieve self-sufficienc in maize production in 1968. There are a number of hard-co problem areas, the most noticeable of which is Barotse Province. While famine can be held in check by importation, this is an unsatisfactory palliative since it necessarily implies high transport cost. For instance, much of Barotse Province's maize supply is produced in the Central Province and carried anything between two and four hundred miles at a cost per bag of about K2–K4. Although the consumer does not normally pay for the transport, it is clearly economically inefficient to have to transport for great distances a high-bulk/low-value product such as maize.

More immediately relevant is the question of diet. We have already seen the President's concern at the inadequate nutritional value of the diet consumed by many in the rural areas. This inadequacy is further evidence of functional inefficiency in the subsistence sector. Its causes are complex, compounded of the absence of males in urban employment, changing values and consumption patterns, and a wide range of ecological factors, of which the most important is undoubtedly the drastic reduction in the availability of game. Although it is no doubt easy to overemphasise the adequacy of the diet in traditional village life, there is evidence that the position has got worse and that in some areas at least nutritional standards have actually fallen over the last 25 or 30 years.

The abuse of land was in the past largely the result of overcrowding following the colonial distribution of lands, and to that extent this particular feature of subsistence or quasi-subsistence agriculture is a heritage of the past. Although expenditure on resettlement schemes has increased since 1964, it is questionable whether the great majority of them are entirely satisfactory in all respects. Thus in some cases the settlement has checked the deterioration of land but has not noticeably improved the standard of living of the people. Nonetheless, it is true that the problem is of much less significance in Zambia than it is for instance in Kenya or Malawi.

Although the subsistence sector, then, is not without its problems, almost by definition agricultural policy must be concerned primarily with those who are gradually leaving the subsistence sector, i.e. those who are selling a proportion of their total output. The numbers of such are rising very rapidly. Although no precise quantitative data are available, the very fact of increasing provincial self-sufficiency in maize, the rising output of maize grown by Africans, and the market opportunities created by increased expenditure in bomas and provincial capitals, all attest to an increasing market awareness on behalf of producers.

Just as the primary concern of the subsistence sector is to produce food for the cultivator, so the primary concern of the commercial or quasi-commercial sector is to produce food for the rest of the economy. In 1966 the value of home-produced food sold in Zambia was K14 million, or about K42 per head of the non-farm population. As population increases and as a larger number of non-farm jobs are created, the value of the agricultural market will rise. Further, as incomes per head rise, the demand for food will grow. Thus the Urban African Budget Survey of 1960 showed that the consumption of foodstuffs by Africans living in towns would rise by slightly over 10n/- for each K2/- increase in wages. This estimate has been shown to be on the low side and the Seers Report of 1962 projected a 41 per cent rise in direct food consumption between 1965 and 1970, and a 40 per cent rise over the same period of sales to other sectors. These projections were, however, based on the assumption of a six per cent per annum rise in gross domestic product over the period, whereas in 1968 the annual growth rate has been nearly three times that assumed by the Seers Report. Thus the First National Development Plan adjusted the Seers projections and showed a twofold rise in private food consumption over the plan period and a three-fold increase in intermediate demand over the same period. Given the assumptions on which the plan projections were based, it is not improbable that these projections will be exceeded. This adds up to a very substantial increase in the demand for food.

Moreover, the problem is not only to increase the quantity of foodstuffs available, but also to adjust the quality of the products to the changing demands of the market. As incomes rise, so the pattern of expenditure changes, with proportionately less money spent on coarser foods and proportionately more spent on luxury foods or more nutritious foods, such as meat, eggs and milk. Comparisons of urban budgets from the surveys of 1960 and 1966 show the extent to which this process has already gone.

It is difficult to exaggerate the impact the rise in demand and the change in the structure of demand has on the agricultural sector. The restructuring of the market necessarily implies a restructuring of the industry, involving the acquisition of new knowledge, the application of new techniques, the production of new crops, the investment of new capital, and the creation of new market structures. This process of restructuring is rendered the more difficult when in the case of Zambia the base of the new industry (e.g. vegetables, poultry, eggs, dairying and pig rearing) is so small. During Federation a large proportion of Zambia's food for direct private consumption came from Southern Rhodesia and even from South Africa, with the result that there was little incentive for the development of specialist intensive units in Zambia. The fact that rising incomes implied both an expansion and a transformation of agricultural production has therefore caught Zambia in an enfilade. This is adequately reflected in the following table, which shows the value of selected foodstuffs imported over the period 1964–1967.

TABLE 1

Imports of selected agricultural commodities 1964–1967

					K to nearest '000	
			1964	1965	1966	1967
Fruit:						
Oranges	..	..	*	3	14	28
Apples	..	..	142	151	95	228
Bananas	..	..	30	35	66	87
			(172)	189	175	343
Vegetables:						
Beans ..	..	..	85	141	182	185
Cabbage	..	..	*	7	13	5
Potatoes	..	..	44	150	242	213
Carrots	..	..	*	6	6	5
			(129)	304	443	408
Dairy Products:						
Eggs (shell) ..	..		68	78	28	54
Milk (powder, full						
cream)	..	..	258	321	462	742
Butter	..	..	366	314	476	263
			692	713	966	1,059
Meats:						
Beef (fresh, frozen and						
chilled)	..	..	347	319	1,311	2,112
Mutton and lamb	..		132	261	302	268
Pork ..	..	..	118	190	352	239
Bacon and ham	..		3	35	304	342
			600	805	2,269	2,961

*not available
Source: *Annual Statements of External Trade*, 1964–1967

It is not adequate to argue that Zambia imports these crops because she is unable to import them at competitive prices. The following Table 2 compares the landed cost of some foodstuffs with the prices obtained by Zambian producers. This shows that in many cases the Zambian producer gets a substantially lower price than the landed cost of the imported article. This amply demonstrates the fact that the cause of imports is not the balance of comparative advantage, but merely the shortage of supply.

TABLE 2

Producer prices and import prices of selected agricultural products 1966

	Average unit price of imports f.o.b.	Computed c.i.f. price[1]	Average producer price, Lusaka
Meat:			
Fresh beef, lb. ..	1/7	1/9	1/5[2]
Dairy Products:			
Eggs in shell, doz. ..	2/6	3/6	3/9
Vegetables:			
Cabbage	4d	6d	5d
Carrots	5d	7d	6d
Peas	8d	9d	8d
Tomatoes	8d	10d	6d
Fruit:			
Oranges, lb.	4d	6d	3d
Pineapples, lb. ..	9d	11d	10d

1. Assumptions. 500-mile haul at cost of 10d/ton/mile. Special rate for eggs.
2. A new price scale was introduced in July 1966. The figure in the Table refers to standard grade under the previous scale and commercial under the new grade.

Source: Important Statistics 1966 and *Monthly Economic Bulletin of Ministry of Agriculture.*

TABLE 3

Consumer price index. Higher and lower incomes, January 1962 100 (Food)

	Combined index	Higher incomes index	Lower incomes index
1960 ..	98.5	97.1	100.6
1961 ..	99.6	98.8	100.9
1962 ..	100.7	99.8	102.1
1963 ..	100.2	99.9	100.6
1964 ..	103.1	102.2	103.7
1965 ..	109.9	106.5	112.7
1966, June	119.6	112.8	126.4
1967, June	124.0	116.1	131.8

Source: Monthly Digest of Statistics.

The domestic supply for such products is highly inelastic in the short run, and the transport bottleneck as well as political considerations ensure the highly inelastic supply of imports. It is inevitable that food prices should rise rapidly. The above extract, Table 3, from the published price indices, show that the price of food has increased by 25 per cent, 1960–1967. At a time when, for quite other reasons, wage levels in Zambia are under great upward pressure, it is clearly undesirable that the cost of living, particularly for low income groups, should rise rapidly. It is no exaggeration to say that the whole development strategy may be vitiated by rapidly rising wages which could be demanded, and partly justified, on the grounds of rising food prices.

But why, it may be asked, is the supply of food so inelastic? One of the main reasons for this is the change in the investment and production policies of the European farming sector. The structure of the industry is exactly what a study of businesses under uncertainty would lead us to expect. There are three marked features. First, an exit from the industry of the politically nervous and, perhaps, the economically uncompetitive. This has led to a slump in the price of land, which is difficult to qualify with any degree of precision: but tales of farms losing more than half their value in the period 1957–1963 are too frequent and widespread to be dismissed lightly. As the possibility of capital loss becomes greater the reluctance to sell of the remaining owners increases. Willy-nilly, they are obliged to remain in the industry. But they protect themselves in ways that explain the remaining two features of the industry. First, their time horizons shorten and they become more like the classical entrepreneur, concerned with short-run profit maximisation. This is borne out by a more intense use of assets (i.e. higher yields per acre) illustrated by the following table:

TABLE 4

Yields per acre of specified crops on European farms, 1961–1966

	1961	*1962*	*1963*	*1964*	*1965*
Virginia flue cured, lbs.	875	957	760	960	886
Burley, lbs.	544	603	622	513	583
Maize—hybrid single, bags	15.1	16.1	13.2	16.1	22
Maize—other, bags ..	13.5	14.8	12.1	15.8	19.2
Cotton, lbs.	333	679	740	1,400	1,056

Source: Agricultural Production Statistics, 1965 (mimeo).

In nearly every case, there has been a fairly strong upward trend in yields per acre, especially in hybrid maize and cotton.

Associated with this rise in yields has been a switch to crops that yield profits quickly, especially maize. The following Table 5, shows how the pattern of cropping has changed, 1954–1965.

TABLE 5

Cropping patterns in selected years, 1954–1965. Value of marketed output

Type of Product	1954	1960	1965
Tobacco	2.9	1.8	2.2
Maize	3.0	1.9	4.1
Potatoes	0.1	0.1	0.1
Other crops	0.3	0.2	0.2
TOTAL CROPS ..	6.3	4.0	6.6
Slaughtered cattle ..	0.8	0.5	0.9
„ pigs	n	0.1	0.1
Dairy Produce	0.6	0.6	0.7
Other Produce	0.2	0.3	0.2
Changes in herd size ..	*	0.5	−0.3
TOTAL LIVESTOCK ..	(1.6)	2.0	1.6
GRAND TOTAL ..	(7.9)	6.0	8.2
Maize as % of Total crops	48%	46%	62%
Maize as % of Grand Total	(38%)	31%	50% .

n=less than 0.1
*not available.
Source: Agricultural Production in Zambia, 1964 (mimeo), and 1965 (mimeo).

The increase in yields per acre and the greater emphasis on maize are symptomatic of a third feature of recent European farming— namely, a failure to invest in immovable assets.

The acreage cleared per year has halved in four years, despite the rapid rise in gross output per cropped acre. Despite a most substantial increase in the demand for fruit and vegetables, the acreage under these capital and labour intensive crops has halved, 1961–1965. It is true that there has been an increase in investment in labour-saving implements—e.g. combine harvesters, shellers and planters. But these are written off over a short period and investment in them is motivated largely by defensive considerations. They reduce the degree of dependence on possibly restive African labour and can sometimes, if necessary, be taken out of the country if the owner decides to migrate south.[1]

Despite attempts, of which the most conspicuous is the paragraphs on large-scale farming in the Plan document, to allay the fears of the European farmers, their insecurity has resulted in a swing to quick, easy crops out of long-run or highly capitalised enterprises. The sale of dairy stock for beef, the elimination of breeding herds, the fall in irrigated acreages and the total cessation of citrus development, are at once symptoms of political uncertainty and causes of imbalances in production.

The second demand on the sector is to produce raw materials for the industrial sector. Type and quantity of such demand will obviously depend upon the overall development strategy being followed in the individual country which in turn will be determined by the natural, human and financial resources available. One of the prime objects of the First National Development Plan is to diversify the economy away from copper towards manufacturing and agriculture. With the transport bottleneck, there is clearly much to be said for the rapid development of agro-industries. But if a significant proportion of industrialisation is based on agricultural input, the quantity and quality of the crop concerned must be assured. This again implies a high degree of investment, technical knowledge, entrepreneurship and commercial skill. So far agro-industries in Zambia have progressed to only a very limited degree. Table 6 shows the low level of intersectoral sales of agriculture in 1965, and the relatively high level of sales of imports from foreign commercial farming, to sectors to which agriculture was selling.

TABLE 6
Intersectoral purchases and imports of agricultural products 1965

	Bought from Zambian commercial farming 1	Bought from foreign commercial Farming 2	$\frac{2}{1}$ %
Slaughteries	160	22	13
Dairies	27	0	—
Grain mills ..	257	57	22
Bakeries	2	0	—
Breweries and tobacco	8	50	625
Other food industries ..	0	9	—
Commercial farming ..	0	23	—

Source: 1965 Matrix.

1. There is an important distinction between investment in mobile assets, which can be removed with little difficulty, and fixed assets, which must be abandoned, written off or sold at a discount in an emergency.

Some of the high values in this table are doubtless explicable technically, e.g. it is not possible to grow hops for brewing beer in Zambia and certain malting sorghums were introduced only in 1967–8. Nonetheless, the balance of the evidence in the table is that the commercial farming sector as a whole was inefficient in producing both for the food industry and for agro-industries. Thus there are no recorded sales to joineries, nor to textiles, though this latter is likely to be corrected when the ginnery and textile mill at Kafue reach full production.

A third function of the agricultural sector is to add to the productive capacity of the community through saving. Given the inadequate base of Zambian agriculture, it is clearly unrealistic to expect a flow of savings from the rural areas to the industrial, such as was achieved in Japan, China and Russia. On the other hand it is not at all unrealistic to expect the agricultural sector as a whole to supply a very considerable part of its own capital. The most basic form this takes is in adding to the stock of productive land through clearing and stumping. There are many other possibilities, e.g. roads, schools, dams, irrigation channels, fencing and anti-erosion works. The concept of seasonal unemployment is now familiar, as is the fact that there is a very substantial investment fund in the agricultural sector, arising from the fact that labour is available during the off season.

The fourth contribution of the agricultural sector is to supply labour to the industrial sector. Typically, as development proceeds, the proportion of the population on the land decreases, so that fewer farmers have to feed more non-farmers. But it is essential that this process be achieved at the right pace. If the agricultural sector is releasing labour to the industrial sector too fast this will lead to urban unemployment; while if the process proceeds too slowly it will lead to a shortage of labour of all kinds in the industrial sector with consequent wage inflation. In Zambia there can be little doubt that the process is proceeding too fast. One of the minor emphases in all the writing on Humanism and in the speech at Mulungushi is the problem of urban drift. While it may be true that the motive force behind this concern is political—for there can be little doubt that a semi-educated core of urban unemployed is a serious threat to political stability—it is equally true that such waste of resources cannot be tolerated in any developing country. Now the causes of urban drift are exceedingly complex and certainly they are not confined to economic factors. On the other hand, there can be little doubt that the huge earnings differential between rural employment in agriculture and urban employment aggravates a problem that would almost certainly exist anyway. There is some tentative evidence that the length of stay in the towns is directly related to the differential between urban earnings and agricultural earnings. Naturally, this varies from area to area and from tribe to tribe. Where a man can earn nearly as much in his village as he can in town, the scanty evidence suggests that his stay in urban employment is short. The effect of rising rural incomes on staunching the flow of labour into the towns is problematical. Be that as it may, the First National Development Plan has naturally given raising rural incomes a high priority and if success to date has been unspectacular, this is inevitable in a notoriously slow-moving part of the economy. Nonetheless, as long as the sector continues to release labour too rapidly, resources are being wasted.

Quantitative data on the rate of urban drift and on the rate of growth of urban unemployment are scarce and unreliable. One estimate puts the figure for 1960–61 at 21,250 migrant job-seekers entering the towns, and for 1963, 16,400. The widening urban/ rural wage differential, the improvements in transport and communications, and the wider opportunities for African employment have probably increased the rate of urban migration since Independence. If Plan targets are met, about 17,000 urban jobs a year will be provided, and to this extent and on the bases of these very unreliable estimates, it is almost certain that the rate of inflow is greater than the rate of job creation. In order to get a measure of additional urban unemployment, one must then allow for job-seekers from the urbanised community. The figure for this in the early 'sixties was roughly 6,000, and therefore the increase in urban unemployment is the excess of the number of immigrant job-seekers, plus those entering the labour market from urban families, minus the number of new jobs created. At a rough guess, the addition to urban unemployment may be something in the region of 8–10,000 a year. This admittedly unreliable figure is a measure of the failure of the agricultural sector in this respect.

The final function of the agricultural sector on the supply side is to be a source of export earnings. In Zambia the rôle of agriculture in this respect, as in that of savings, is obscured by the economic impact of the copper industry. Thus in 1966, agriculture exported slightly under K8 million worth of produce compared with copper's K480 million. In some ways a more relevant comparison, agricultural exports would have paid for less than four per cent of total imports. While from the point of view of balance of payments this should cause increasing concern, the more important perspective is that of the loss of rural income implied by lost export opportunities. Given Zambia's natural endowment, there is little doubt that agricultural exports, particularly in beef, tobacco, fruit and groundnuts, could be substantially increased in the long run. This again implies a restructuring of the industry, a substantial increase in output and vastly improved marketing facilities.

On the demand side the sector's prime function is to be a market for products of the industrial sector. The increases in output, which we have discussed in terms of supply, create increases in rural income: this rising rural income is then spent on home-produced goods from the industrial sector. The interdependence of the two sectors is therefore close. It could be argued that since Zambia suffers from demand inflation, any increase in demand from the rural areas would merely add to the inflationary pressures already in the economy. Even if rural demand were to spill over into imports, this would merely aggravate transport bottlenecks. Therefore, so it could be argued, rural demand should be held down rather than increased. In the short run, i.e. while the more acute bottlenecks, principally transport and manpower, remain, there is doubtless some truth in this view. But rising standards of living in the rural areas are a pre-condition of rapid agricultural transformation. Indeed, there can be little doubt that one of the most potent agents in the process of agricultural change is improved consumption patterns and the demonstration effect often associated with it. Further, it is clearly socially and politically undesirable that rural expenditures, already low, should be held down by shortage of supply in order to make room for urban and government demand. It could even be argued that what is required is the release of resources currently used in satisfying luxury demands in both goverment and urban sectors, for the rapid expansion of supply of non-luxury goods for satisfaction of demand in the rural areas. Precisely this argument is now being employed in Tanzania. However, in Zambia there is little evidence yet of rural demand being sufficiently substantial to add significantly to inflationary pressures in the economy. In 1965 gross domestic product of commercial farming, which includes non-African farming plus sales from African farming, valued at factor cost, was fractionally over K16 million. If we assume that the average propensity to consume home-produced goods and services is 0·4, then the demand for home-produced goods arising from the agricultural sector as a whole was about K6·5 million, or about one per cent of gross national product. If the whole of the K6·5 million had been spent on the products of the manufacturing sector, even then 85 per cent of the population in the rural areas would have bought less than 20 per cent of the total output of the manufacturing sector. In a sense, therefore, the sectors are hardly interdependent; and although it may be true at the moment that there is no need to increase demand on the non-agricultural sectors, it is unlikely that the agrarian revolution looked for in the philosophy of Humanism will get under way until the flow of goods into the rural areas is much more substantial than it is at present.

Humanism and agricultural development

We must now ask how far Humanism and its implications is relevant to these fundamental problems. We have seen that the most serious bottleneck to agricultural development is capital—seasonal, short-term and long-term credit and infrastructural capital. Both the *Guide to the Implementation* and the Mulungushi speech emphasise that one solution to the shortage of capital is the substitution of cheap productive assets for expensive ones: more specifically, oxen for tractors. This substitution allows the motive power bottleneck to be breached if not abolished for more farm families with given resources, and thereby helps remove the spectre of individual farm capitalists. Given Zambia's disappointing experience of mechanisation and the emphasis hitherto placed upon the principle of acreage extension through "tractorisation", the President's new emphasis on ox-cultivation is pure gain. But it merely raises in another, perhaps diluted, form a question that has haunted agricultural policy-makers the world over, and in Zambia particularly since the early years of this decade. Put crudely, the issue is this: given scarce resources, is not the optimum allocation to those with the highest marginal product? Classical welfare economics leaves the issue in no doubt. But is classical welfare economics the right tool to apply? The limitations of its assumptions and the restricted socio-economic milieu of its development unfit it to answer such questions in an entirely different environment. Politically, too, it is dangerous to favour a minority which is already "emergent". In Zambia this debate has been going on within the Ministry of Agriculture for five years. What is Humanism's contribution to it?

The antipathy towards individual capitalism, towards the profit motive and towards "the price tag economy" makes it clear that the conclusion of welfare economics is not acceptable. Humanism implies a concern for *all* men, irrespective of marginal productivities. Traditional society did not reject the inadequte or ineffective: rather it sought to mobilise the abilities they did have. But the objection stands that resources *are* scarce: there simply are not enough agricultural extension workers, financial resources and transport subsidies to realise the implications of Humanism universally. Indeed, the indiscriminate distribution of credit in 1966–7 and the record of repayment reveal the extent of the problem in this crucial area. There is a way out of this dilemma: it will be discussed in the last section.

If the problem of distribution of scarce (capital) resources thus remains largely unsolved, the twin problem of capital *creation* is hardly touched. The irony of capital starvation amidst potential capital abundance is a commonplace of development economics. Even in well-developed agricultural regions, the average household has ample spare labour capacity from June to October. Here is a vast potential source of capital. The spare labour could build dams, improve roads, dig irrigation channels, clear land and add greatly to the productive capacity of the village or community if it were properly mobilised. In mobilisation lies the key. But mobilisation requires motivation: and motivation requires inspiration. India, China, Russia, even Colombia, Chile and Algeria have shown what can be achieved if spare labour capacity can be inspired—or compelled, in some cases—to create capital. *Ujamaa* has this inspiration. Humanism so far has not.

President Kaunda is aware of the necessity of using spare labour, for example, to construct irrigation works:

"Billions and billions of gallons of water are running away from us every minute to the oceans . . . Properly organised village committees can co-ordinate their activities in such a way that they would trap this priceless gem."

He sees the party as providing the inspiration, motivation and organisation. The last it can do well, where the local leadership is strong. Very occasionally it has shown it can provide the inspiration, but it is here that the contrast between *Ujamaa* and humanism is most marked. Indeed, some features of the humanist philosophy as presented by President Kaunda positively obstruct this process. By presenting as the ideal to which modern village life should move the stagnant society of traditional Zambia, the ideal type of humanism conflicts with the means by which that type will have to be achieved. No doubt this is to distort the President's vision: but the concept of a mutual aid society, particularly when presented as a rediscovery of the values of the past, is in danger of lacking the dynamism necessary to mobilise the disguised saving in the rural areas.

As far as the functional inefficiency of the agricultural sector is concerned, the production policies that arise out of Humanism are clearly consistent with the search for a more balanced output mix. Import substitution can cover agro-industrial imports as well as foodstuffs. The food and industrial input criteria are therefore well covered by Humanist thinking. Capital creation has already been discussed.

Labour, market and export criteria thus remain. We have already seen that urban drift constitutes one of the biggest social problems of present-day Zambia. Humanism therefore emphasises the need to improve the quality of life in the rural areas—hence the stress laid upon village regrouping and the provision of social amenities. The attempts to bring the benefits of an urban environment to the rural areas are bold but possibly misplaced. The causes of urban drift are complex and imperfectly understood—but it is at best unlikely that the provision of some social facilities would greatly affect the rate of labour transfer even if village regrouping were universal. We must not, however, confuse means and ends. The object of village regrouping is not *only* to provide counter-attractions to the towns: the humanist would emphasise that the provision of a wider range of facilities that regrouping makes possible is a desirable end in itself and should be judged accordingly.

Accepting that, does Humanism offer any further insight into this problem? In one way it does. Humanism has its philosophical roots in rural society and obliges planners and politicians to take seriously the claims upon them of the rural community. The First

National Development Plan, for instance, anticipated the emphasis on rural development by allocating 65 per cent of total capital investment over the Plan period to the rural areas. This is significant, since the most promising approach to the reduction of urban drift is to close the urban/rural income gap. This implies heavy investment in agriculture (even at the expense of industrial expansion) and an improvement in the terms of trade of the agricultural sector *vis-à-vis* the industrial sector. This latter implies a relative rise in foodstuff prices and is discussed below. If Humanism can create a political climate in which the diversion of investment from the industrial sector to the agricultural sector and the deterioration of the industrial sector's internal terms of trade can be accepted and even welcomed, then it will have made a genuine contribution to correcting this particular form of functional inefficiency.

The market criterion is clearly related to the rate of growth of incomes in the rural sector, which is determined by the rate of growth of output and the prices of agricultural produce; to this extent, we have already discussed Humanism's impact on the rôle of the agricultural sector as an internal market, in so far as it affects investment and the terms of trade. One further point needs discussion. The agricultural sector can be a market for home-produced goods only in so far as it is served by an efficient rural distribution network. By forcibly and, some may claim, prematurely Zambianising rural distribution, it is arguable that the President has jeopardised the chances of rapid development of and demand for the products of the industrial sector. It is too early to judge. The obvious danger is that as relatively inexperienced and under-capitalised Zambian retailers take over rural distribution, the "demonstration effect" in agricultural production and the effective demand for home-produced goods will both be reduced. Thus there is at least a danger that two objectives—higher standards of living in the rural areas and commercial opportunities for Zambians —may temporarily be in conflict.

The seeds of conflict are also evident in the fulfilment of the export criterion. The diversification of the economy necessarily implies a significant increase in the exports of the agricultural sector, which in turn implies increased production of exportable produce, notably tobacco and groundnuts. This clearly conflicts with the food criterion which demands the rapid switching of resources from maize to other food crops, beef and fruit. In the long term, it may well be possible, with the widespread adoption of irrigation, to follow Kenya's example of developing a considerable export trade in food crops and meat. For the next ten years, however, given current rates of increase in the demand for food, it is unlikely that agricultural resources will be adequate rapidly to develop production of both food and export crops. Government is thus faced with a difficult decision. Humanism requires that the former be given priority: economic structuralism demands that the latter have priority.[1]

Finally, we may ask what Humanism implies for the European commercial farmer. We have seen how political nervousness is reflected in farm management decisions and the undesirable effects these have on the sector as a whole. The problem is real. For in its antagonism to capitalism, its emphasis on the right of Zambians to a real economic rôle in their own country, its insistence on State ownership of land and its condemnation of landowners who do not exploit their land, Humanism can hold little comfort for those who are conditioned to see political threats in every utterance. Bland assurances that the country needs large-scale farmers or philosophical treatises on the value of the individual are unlikely to convince the politically neurotic. If the country really does need large-scale European farmers, policies must be formulated that will convince them of Government's intentions. Cliché though it be, actions speak louder than words.

Filling the policy gap

We must now turn from the discussion of the extent to which Humanism recognises the basic problem to deal with the question of the policy gap. In the introduction to this essay we stressed that Humanism is, as it were, a proximate ethic which lays down general insights but does not often give specific policy proposals. It is beyond the scope of an essay of this length to detail policies in every department of agriculture. All that can be done is to suggest some possible policies that would at once be faithful to the spirit of Humanism and grapple with some of the central problems. The first basic problem is that of the distribution of scarce resources. If this problem is allied with that of the increase in those resources

---

1. This is slightly oversimplified. So long as the former implies import substitution, structuralists can have no objection. Only when resources are diverted from exports to increased home consumption is there a real conflict.

through capital creation by the mobilisation of spare labour capacity, then a joint solution emerges. If Government-controlled resources are distributed to those who are most ready to create additional capital resources themselves, then there results both an incentive to such capital creation and an assurance that whereas all individuals and communities have an equal or nearly equal claim on resources, only those who have shown sufficient enterprise and self-sacrifice to maximise returns to Government's resources receive them. To some extent this is already accepted policy. For instance, in education the ministry accepts responsibility for schools that are built by local communities on a self-help basis. There seems to be everything to be said from the point of view both of Humanism and from the point of view of traditional economic theory for a much wider application of this technique to the problems of resource distribution. The stimulation of the creation of productive capacity in the rural areas by the mobilisation of savings already apparent in them must have a high priority. As far as manpower is concerned, this technique may not increase the stock of skilled manpower, but it does suggest the means by which skilled manpower can be allocated. Rather than waste this crucial resource by scattering it thinly over all provinces, it would be both more efficient and consistent with the basic concepts of Humanism to make adequate manpower resources available to those communities which were most ready to add to their own productive capacity. If it be said that this entails making the rich richer, it must be accepted that there is an element of truth in this. But since the additional wealth of productive assets will be created by the communities themselves, rather than being the inheritance of the past or unearned benefits, it would be more accurate to say that the policy here advocated is one of giving help to those who have shown that they are ready to help themselves. There is nothing new or revolutionary in this policy, but it is to be contrasted with the sorry history of handouts of Government largesse which one respected observer, at any rate, feels have done more harm than good by conditioning people in the rural areas to look to central government for all their needs. The agrarian revolution, to which Humanism looks, can never be accomplished while such attitudes persist.

We turn now to a consideration of production policies. It is perhaps in this area that the gap between the ends that are consistent with Humanism and the means by which the end can be achieved is greatest. Nor is it surprising, since the normal method of effecting changes in the pattern of production is through differential prices. The problems here are two. First, there is sufficient evidence that for many traditional producers the supply curve is negatively inclined: that is, that as the price rises less is produced. This is particularly true in the case of cattle. If, therefore, a high priority is to be given to an increase in the production of cattle by the traditional producers, this necessarily implies a fall in the price. However, since the supply curves of commercial farmers, again, say, for beef, are positively inclined, i.e. more is supplied as price increases, the maximisation of the rate of increase of supply entails lower prices for some producers and higher prices for others. This is obviously politically unacceptable, particularly given the broad racial division between commercial producers and traditional producers. If price is going to be retained as the arbiter of output it is thus necessary to ensure that producers react to price changes in broadly the same way. Before we look at the problem posed by changing producers' reactions to price changes, we ought perhaps to ask whether price should be accepted as the only arbiter of output.

The President is highly critical of what he calls the price-tag economy. He would therefore be happy to see the substitution of other forces for price as the determinant of output. The most obvious alternative is political, and that is the mobilisation of resources through political persuasion and cajoling. Two points are in order in this respect. First, where political pressures have been tried in other countries, they have not been notably successful. In India, Egypt, and even in Russia, the attempt to use the Party as a means of securing economic and agricultural change has resulted more in weakening of the party than in the acceleration of agricultural development. Second, village production councils, as outlined in the *Guide to the Implementation*, are likely to be successful only if they can make available to producers both the incentive to produce and the means of production. Persuasion and leadership doubtless have a part to play, but such evidence as we have on the behaviour of small-scale farmers in Zambia suggests that they are more likely to respond to calls for higher levels of production or entry into different crops if they are assured of a market, and if they have all the resources necessary to produce. Political pressure in any form is unlikely to be successful unless the basic economic pre-conditions are met.

Political pressures may be helpful in changing the producer's reaction to change in price. If producers can be persuaded to react positively to changes in price then the problem of changing agricultural output becomes that much easier. However, it is likely that a more potent force in thus changing producers' reactions is availability of consumer goods. Although perhaps in conflict with the spirit if not the letter of some of President Kaunda's writing on Humanism, it seems realistic to suppose that as the standard of living rises and as patterns of consumption change, so the reaction to increased prices changes from that of the target worker to that of the commercial producer. If this is true, it implies an improvement in rural retail distribution. As we have already seen, at Mulungushi the President announced that these would be taken over very rapidly by Zambians. While there is general agreement with the desire to see Zambians play a much larger part in the economic life of the nation, it is essential to ensure that the range of goods offered in the rural areas and the service provided by the retailers are sufficient to induce rural producers to enter more fully into the money economy. The rural retail sector can thus play a significant part not only in increasing agricultural production, but also in accelerating the rural sector's entry into the market for industrial goods. This provides a further base for industrialisation in the future.

The advantage of universal positive price elasticity of supply is clearly that it enables the Government to pursue price policies that will transform, in time, the output patterns of the agricultural sector. This implies that for most products the Government will have to raise prices, or allow prices to rise, to a significant degree. Only in the case of maize may it be necessary to reduce the price in order to eliminate embarrassing surpluses. This improvement in the terms of trade of agriculture *vis-à-vis* the rest of the economy and imports which we have already discussed in another context obviously implies in its turn a rise in the cost of living for the urban population. This seems to be the cost of the prime objectives of Humanism, namely rapidly rising standards of living in the rural areas and large-scale import substitution. Firm wage control or a series of planned devaluations is thus inevitable if this approach to agricultural development is to be accepted. The myth that rapid agricultural development can coexist with a long-run deterioration in agricultural terms of trade has been adequately exploded, but it will take political courage to face the consequences of fast-rising food prices.

We now turn to problems of agricultural organisation. Normally this would be seen as a subsidiary issue, since it would be argued that what is important is the standard of living in the agricultural sector, and the institutional framework within which that standard of living is improved is of minor significance. However, we have already emphasised that Humanism is concerned with the standard of living as only one component of the wider concept of the quality of life, and it therefore follows that it sees the form of productive organisation as a variable quite as important as the standard of living. As already indicated, President Kaunda lays much emphasis on the virtues of co-operatives as combining individual initiative with mutual interdependence. However, the extent to which co-operative organisation offers a morally or spiritually superior life than individual enterprise is largely determined by the success of the co-operative. If there are delays, difficulties, frustrations and losses, even the most ardent co-operators soon become disenchanted. From this it follows that, as the Dumont Report emphasised, the pace of the formation of co-operatives must be closely related to the resources available. The wholesale establishment of co-operatives without adequate credit, technical help and marketing structures is simply a recipe for disaster. The impression to be gained from visits to co-operatives in Zambia at the moment is that the more specialist the co-operative the more successful it has been. Thus, poultry and vegetable co-operatives, admittedly with a strong though disorganised market, have been fairly successful, while those based on more varied production patterns have been proportionately less successful. This suggests that one way forward is to use specialist co-ops as poles of growth for given economic regions. The further development of this would be to group specialist co-operatives, particularly where they are practising intensive forms of production, around resettled or regrouped villages, in order that the specialist knowledge acquired by the co-operators may be shared over as wide a range as possible. Clearly, this has the additional advantage of economising on scarce skilled manpower in two ways. First, since a number of distinct but related co-operatives could be founded within one area, one or two technical assistants could be more effectively employed advising the co-operatives than would be the case if the co-operatives were scattered over a large area. Secondly, since the co-operators themselves will acquire technical knowledge, they can become voluntary or even paid extension workers, helping the individual producers in the area with their problems. The grouping of co-operatives could also have technical advantages, e.g. poultry co-operatives could sell manure to vegetable co-operatives, which in turn could sell crop residues to the poultry co-operatives. The greater the degree of mutual interdependence between the co-operatives themselves, and between the co-operatives on the one hand and the individual producers on the other, the more consistent the organisation becomes with the ideals of Humanism.

But if co-operatives are to be grouped in this way they must be grouped in reasonable proximity to fairly substantial markets, e.g. bomas, provincial headquarters, regrouped villages, or the line of rail. This implies that the development of co-operatives in the more remote areas will have to be more gradual. Since in many of these areas the breakdown of the traditional way of life has been slow and therefore has gone less far, this need not be too serious; on the other hand much can be done to strengthen group activity and preserve the better features of the mutual aid society by encouraging villages, even in the most distant parts, to undertake communal capital creation projects. Although the difficulties of this should not be underestimated, the fact that traditional authority structures and traditional ideals are more intact in the remoter areas should remove some of the problems that are likely to be encountered in areas in which the traditional ethos has largely evaporated.

So far we have been primarily concerned with that section of the agricultural sector which is slowly emerging from a pure subsistence type of farming to full commercial farming. We must now turn to large-scale commercial farming, that is, almost exclusively European farming. The First National Development Plan rightly recognises the fact that the continuation and expansion of the sub-sector is a necessary pre-condition of economic development in Zambia as a whole. We have also seen how the European farm sector has reacted to political and economic changes over the last few years, by taking up defensive and, in broad terms, undesirable production and investment policies. To this extent the European farming community poses a substantial challenge to the whole of the philosophy of Humanism. For it is necessary to convince the thousand or so European commercial farmers that they are not excluded from the vision of a Humanistic society. Although many of the ideals of a Humanist society are foreign to them, they must not be allowed to think that the search for such a society entails their displacement. Failure on this score will mean a rapid deterioration in the efficiency of the sector as a whole. What practical policies, then, can be adopted to ensure that, within the philosophical and political boundaries of Humanism, it remains productive and that European farmers are prepared again to take a longer view of their operation? The first thing that is essential is that they be given grounds for confidence in the future of the country, and of their place in it. One possible way of doing this would be to offer them a guaranteed price for their farms related to earnings. Provided the price was based on a sufficiently long series of earnings there would be little fear of abuse of the land, and since the value of the land would be determined by its output, there would be every incentive to increase the productivity of the land. A policy such as this could go a considerable way towards revolutionising the investment and production policies of the large-scale commercial farmers. Further, differential weights could be attached to different crops in order to provide an incentive to switching out of questionably economic (from a national point of view) crops such as maize to high value crops such as cotton or tobacco.

This price guarantee could be made conditional upon the European farmers playing their part in the agrarian revolution. The European farming community is a rich resource of experience, skill and technical ability. It is right that these resources be utilised for the benefit of the community as a whole. This entails mobilising these resources by encouraging the Europeans to play their part in the training and supervision of emergent Zambian farmers. Two possibilities suggest themselves. First, those European farmers near large markets could supervise groups of co-operatives and in the first instance train two or three co-operators from each enterprise to a fairly high level of skill. In return for a guaranteed earnings-related selling price for their farms, therefore, European farmers would increase the rate at which the co-operative movement could advance. The other possibility is that European farmers not situated in a favourable location for the development of groups of co-operatives could undertake the training of a given number of

Zambian farmers in the same way that a small number of more liberally minded European farmers are already doing on a voluntary basis. Providing that the training requirement were carefully tailored to each individual and his enterprise, and that there were some means of ensuring that the training requirements were, in fact, fulfilled, a scheme such as this could integrate large-scale commercial farmers into the agrarian revolution in a way that would be beneficial both to themselves and to the community at large.

Conclusion

In summary conclusion, we have tried to show that Humanism must be considered in a wider context than that of classical welfare economics. It is concerned with the quality of life of the whole population and not just the standard of living of the most productive fraction. This means that the criteria which the economist is accustomed to employ are often inapplicable or partial, and he must therefore speak with due humility and restraint. Nonetheless, it is important to detect those areas in which inconsistencies can occur without vigorous priority-rating. We have suggested that in both production policies and farm organisation there are potential conflicts which can only be solved by political decisions. In some cases—e.g. the distribution of scarce resources in agriculture—the philosophical base of Humanism provides little help in making difficult decisions: only further reflection and creative political dialogue can fill this vacuum.

Further study and thought is thus required. But no less important is the inspiration that alone can mobilise Zambia's vast rural resources. Hitherto, the motivation has been solely profit, personal gain. If Humanism seeks to dispense with profit, it must replace it with an even more powerful *force motif*. This is the greatest challenge facing the agricultural revolutionaries today, not only in Zambia, but throughout Africa, most of Latin America and parts of South-East Asia. We search for a third way between the spiritually corrosive motives of capitalism and the dehumanising forces of totalitarianism. The contribution of Zambian Humanism to this quest thus has not only a local significance: it could come to have global importance.

7

LABOUR AND ZAMBIAN HUMANISM

Kevin P Quinn, SJ*

There are three different but interrelated meanings given to the term "labour". The first is basic and equates labour with "work". The second describes a particular type of worker, one who works for another, usually under a contract of employment. The third use is a collective noun to denote employed workers organised in trade unions and forming the main portion of what is called the Labour Movement. I propose to deal with these three aspects of labour and to show how they have a part to play in the implementation of Humanism in Zambia.

Zambian society a society of work

The original unit of Zambian society, a tribe or a village, was a society of labour. Each family tilled the land, hunted or fished and almost completely by its own work produced the goods and services that are the material basis of social life. The Gross Domestic Product of the country was the sum total of all that was produced by the individual families. There was no problem in the sharing of the Domestic Product among the people. Apart from a certain share due to the local chief, what a family produced was its share in the Product. Further, its right to that share was the fact that it had worked in its production.

While this form of economic activity should not be romanticised —it was a hard life—it did have certain characteristics that deserve attention. First of all it was a family effort. Hence all, men and women, young and old played their due part in production. In this it differs from present-day paid employment in which, owing

---

*FATHER KEVIN P. QUINN, S.J., Senior Lecturer in Economics at the University of Zambia. Member of several Commissions of Inquiry into labour problems in Zambia, including the *Brown Commission*. Chairman of Wages Council for the Hotel and Catering Industry.

chiefly to the lack of opportunities for paid work open to women, one person is responsible for the upkeep of all his dependants. The institution of the extended family often makes an urban worker responsible for a wide circle of relatives.

A second characteristic is that the family effort took place inside a social framework of co-operation and mutual aid among one's neighbours. This resulted in a fairly egalitarian society with no great discrepancies between rich and poor. All suffered equally if a crop failed or herds were wiped out by disease. It may not have provided a very high standard of living but it did stress that work was the source of material well-being. This is, as I hope to show, a key factor in the implementation of a really Zambian Humanism.

One could write extensively on what some writers call "the philosophy of work", but it is enough here simply to recall the obvious. Whatever gifts and resources Nature may have given to a country, by themselves they will not be of benefit to men. Man must work on and with these resources. Through this work a man benefits not just himself and his family, he also confers benefits on his fellow workers and even on future generations by building up skills and communicating them to others, by creating real capital in the form of factories, machines, cleared land, better cattle. Work can be summed up as the means by which men working with Nature's gifts make their world a better place to live in. It hardly needs stressing that by work I do not mean just crude physical labour: I mean man's intelligence directing the physical powers of Nature, so that Nature works with man instead of against him. The worker of today requires the technology of today in order to make his labour as productive as possible.

One of the main methods of implementing Zambian Humanism is to give to the people of the rural areas modern agricultural techniques so that their production per head increases. This will enable them to have a larger surplus to dispose of in the money economy and so have cash to buy the products of industry. I am not advocating the introduction of new techniques merely because they are new. The techniques introduced should be adapted to the requirements of the soil and the absorptive capacity of the rural population.

The need to increase the productivity of the work of the rural farming is immediately evident from the fact that family work is still the sole means of acquiring economic goods and services for the vast majority of the population of Zambia. Over 450,000 families are engaged in subsistence agriculture and in 1966 their consumption was just over K40m. Since they consume most of their product this means that consumption equals income and so the rural population has an annual income per family of approximately K90.

Paid employment in the money economy

Until the middle of the twenties subsistence farming was universal in Zambia. The Zambian's contact with wage employment was almost exclusively confined to working as an agricultural labourer for European commercial farmers. Apart from employment by the government as messengers, clerks and teachers the two main sources of employment were the lead mine at Kabwe and the railways. Zambia was a reservoir of labour for the mines of South Africa and Katanga and for agriculture and mining in Southern Rhodesia. The development of copper mining in Zambia in the thirties transformed the whole economy. The number of Africans in paid employment increased fairly steadily until in 1966 it was over 300,000.

The bulk of the 300,000 are in a relatively small section of the country—along the line of rail from Livingstone to the Congo border. The chief sectors in which they are engaged are: building and construction 74,000, mining and quarrying 48,000, agriculture, forestry and fisheries 35,000, services (other than Domestic Service) 50,000, manufacturing 29,000, transport and communication 18,000. (*Source: Monthly Digest of Statistics*, March 1968, p. 2.) This growth of paid employment is a useful indicator of the extent to which Zambia has moved over towards being a money economy. Another useful indicator is the growth of the Gross Domestic Product of the money economy. In 1938 it was roughly K24m, K68m in 1948, K245m in 1958 and in 1966 it was K600m. (*Source:* All figures except those for 1966: *National Accounts and Balance of Payments of Northern Rhodesia, Nyasaland and Southern Rhodesia 1954–63*, C.S.O., Salisbury, 1964, Table 49, p. 49. 1966 figures are based on "Gross Domestic Product by Industry", Table 54, *Monthly Digest of Statistics*, March 1968, p. 52. From the total G.D.P. at Factor Cost I have subtracted the G.D.P. of "Other farming, forestry and fishing").

Dualism of the Zambian economy

One could describe the condition of present-day Zambia as being that of a "dual economy". The bulk of the population is outside the money economy. The money economy does, however, affect rural life in a very definite manner. Paid employment has become the goal of all ambitious young men and women. Hence, in spite of an acute housing shortage and the relatively few job openings for the unskilled, the youth of the rural areas are flocking into the towns. The effect of this in some rural areas is that agriculture is left to the old, the women and the very young and so productivity does not increase. No firm figures are available concerning the number of unemployed in the towns but it is undoubtedly far higher than the number who register as unemployed, who in January 1968 numbered 11,500. Urban unemployment has become a major social problem.

When one turns to the earnings of those in employment another "dualism" appears—the gap between African workers and others (mostly Europeans). In 1966 the average annual earnings of all Africans were K480 while those of others were K4,090. There was a wide spread in earnings ranging from K190 for Africans and K3,040 for others in agriculture to K934 and K6,598 respectively in mining and quarrying. In order of rank below mining were the following sectors (the first figure is African earnings, the second others): transport and communications K688, K4,462; services K526, K2,736; commerce K488, K2,898; manufacturing K478, K3,556; electricity, water sanitary services K456, K4,928. (*Source: Monthly Digest of Statistics*, March 1968, Table 4, p. 4). The differences between rural incomes and those of the urban employed and between African and other employed are certainly a big contrast to the relatively egalitarian pre-industrial Zambia. Modern Zambia can be divided into two main groups—the haves and the have-nots (the rural community). The haves can be subdivided into the have-some (Africans) and the have-a-lot (others).

Rôle of the Trade Unions in the past

One of the main factors leading to the differences between Africans and others and between Africans themselves has been the activity of strongly organised trade unions. Naturally at the beginning of industrialization the Africans' lack of experience and skills plus the necessity of importing skilled labour from abroad meant that there was a wide gap in the earnings of the two groups. With the course of time the African became a stable worker, gained experience and a certain degree of skill but the gap in earnings widened because the others, chiefly Europeans in mining and the railways, organised themselves into unions and particularly after 1945 were able to win large wage increases. In the mines the European unions in addition got from the companies the right to represent practically all semi-skilled workers and as the African advanced up the ladder of promotion the European union insisted that he should be paid the "rate for the job", i.e. European rate of pay. This in effect closed the door on African advancement.

When Africans formed their own trade unions most of their efforts were devoted to breaking down the barriers to promotion and in obtaining higher pay and better conditions of work for their members. The various stages of this struggle are recorded in the reports of several commissions of inquiry and the history of that struggle is recounted in Part I of the Brown Report (1966). The trade unions deserve great credit for their achievements in winning justice for their members but there were certain consequences that have made it more difficult to carry Humanism into effect in Zambia.

The first of these is that for the social cohesion of the earlier Zambian society there was substituted the solidarity of workers based on their industrial function. The employed became conscious of their unity not just as workers but as miners, railway workers, builders, etc. The second is that as the methods of operation of unions and the trade union legislation were based on British models the regulation of industrial relations was primarily the affair of the parties concerned, namely the employers and the workers through their unions. The Government took no direct part; its rôle was confined to providing labour officers and other services aimed at avoiding a complete rupture between workers and employers. The right to strike and its excercise were the weapons of the unions. Only if the public were greatly inconvenienced did the Government go further by setting up various *ad hoc* bodies, such as commissions of inquiry. Such bodies had not the legal authority to secure the acceptance of their decisions and recommendations. Hence their recommendations were usually practical compromises whose objective was generally short term. There were so many commissions, however, particularly in mining, that the resulting system of wages and of general industrial relations was a hotch-potch of disparate elements. This was unfortunate because the wages and conditions determined in mining became the norm for workers in other industries. This is usually referred to as the "wage spread". It is particularly important today when owing to a shortage of semi-skilled and skilled labour the wages and conditions in the prosperous industries tend to become those generally demanded and got by workers in other industries and in government. To quote one example of this the Brown Commission's (1966) recommendation of a 22 per cent increase for all Zambians in mining was soon followed by a somewhat similar award by the Whelan Commission for government employees.

It is quite understandable that the African trade unions aimed at obtaining European wages and conditions. These, however, were built on an artificial basis of scarcity and strong union power and could be paid only by fairly prosperous industries; consequently it does not necessarily follow that such a high level of wages could be supported by other industries and by the whole economy especially when, after Independence, the Government began its drive for economic development. This changed the economy from being just a few export-orientated industries and an import sector aimed at catering for European consumption. Its place is being taken by an integrated economy aimed at developing the potential of the whole country for all the people. The high level of wages could be an obstacle to setting up new industries. It has in fact led many employers to make use of fairly capital-intensive methods and so fewer people are able to get employment.

Since ownership and supervision in industry were usually foreign the Zambian worker did not feel any sense of identification with his employer. He had little incentive to be interested in productivity or in helping in the development of industry. Hence the trade unions tended to concentrate their attention on the division of the national cake rather than on making the cake bigger. On the other hand foreign employers did not necessarily have the well-being of the country at heart and so there was lacking a sense of unity of purpose between employers and workers that is essential for the success of a system of industrial relations based on co-operation and agreement.

The previous paragraphs should not be taken as implying that the Zambian trade unions were at fault or should have acted differently. In the actual circumstances of the time they could hardly have done otherwise. But methods and attitudes formed in the past tend to become permanent. They are not thereby the most desirable ones when the whole economy is being changed radically. Zambian Humanism calls for co-operation rather than conflict, national rather than sectional interests, productivity rather than just dividing up a small national cake. The task of trade union leaders is to create a new outlook among their members.

It may seem to the reader that this essay has been excessively descriptive and historical. Up to this point it has said practically nothing about Humanism. That has been done deliberately. Unless one takes account of the existing condition of things efforts to change them for the better are liable to fail. The carrying out of Humanism requires that we are clear in our own minds on the main points of difference between the earlier form of Zambian society and the present industrial society. What is required is not a return to the past but an infusion of the past ideals into modern institutions and structure. For this reason I now pull together in a short synthesis the changes that have happened through the introduction of a money economy.

Differences between subsistence and money economy

The first and most fundamental change is that whereas the subsistence economy depended on the co-operation and mutual aid of one's immediate neighbours in the village or tribe, the modern economy depends on the co-operation of all the groups and sections in the nation. This scarcely requires proof. The recent transport strikes show how much the various parts of the economy are interdependent. A stoppage in copper mining results in less revenue to the government and smaller foreign earnings, while its effects are seen in a slowing down of economic activity and so we get fewer hospitals and schools. As economic development goes ahead this interdependence grows because the economy becomes more integrated. In fact economists often use the extent of integration as an indicator of the stage of development.

Concomitant with integration is specialisation. Whereas the subsistence farmers produced almost everything they required a modern economy calls for division of labour. This in turn often places small groups in so strong a position that they can win disproportionate benefits for themselves. Only by a return to the old spirit of mutual aid and co-operation can Zambia avoid being held up to ransom by relatively small groups. As specialisation proceeds it becomes increasingly hard for the individual to see how his particular task is of benefit to so many others, especially as unlike the village economy he is not bound to them by social and family ties.

To secure the co-operation of the individual worker it is not enough to tell him that he should do so because now Zambia is an independent nation. He must be helped to see that his work and his sacrifices do better others. This can only be done by educating the worker in the realities of Zambia's economic life. This is a task that pertains to the Government, the unions and even to employers. I do not propose to elaborate on this point here but the communication of knowledge between workers and management is an important aspect of industrial relations. Various techniques are available in getting across this vital information at the level of the individual, of the department and of the firm; it must also be conveyed through works and industrial councils. To know what a worker should do does not ensure that he does it. He must be convinced that all others in the industry and in the economy are making sacrifices proportionate to their status and incomes. Finally he must be given a strong stimulus by appeals to patriotism or idealism; the examples of Israel, China and the early revolutionary Russia show how potent such appeals can be.

The second major change from a subsistence economy is that personal work is no longer one's title to a share in the national product. A man gets his share of the product not by producing it but by having the money to buy it. Since our economy is one of exchange a man gets this money either by selling something that he has produced or selling something that he has, namely his labour. I do not propose here to enter into the pros and cons of the benefits of an exchange economy but it is beyond dispute that in Zambia it has resulted in a vast increase in the amount of goods and services available each year. An exchange economy does not, however, secure automatically that these goods are equitably distributed among the whole population. The figures of earnings quoted earlier indicate that there are wide disparities in Zambia.

By accepting an exchange economy Zambia is richer than under a subsistence economy. But there are certain consequences that arise. Many people, chiefly the young, the women, the aged and handicapped, are no longer in a position to make an active contribution to the national product. They must be supported by others. Since the communal spirit of the village scarcely exists in the towns the burden of supporting them should fall on the actively engaged labour force. Hence it is inevitable that there will be an increase in social services. Those in employment should look on the cost of these services as the price that must be paid for the increased flow of goods that results from an exchange economy. Society cannot claim these benefits unless it is ready to help those who through no fault of their own cannot acquire the means of sharing in the greater prosperity. Every Zambian is his brother's keeper.

Since money is the means or title by which a person secures his share in the national product society owes it to every able-bodied individual that he should be able to find employment or to produce something that earns a money income. It is imperative that Zambia widen the job opportunities for as many as possible of its citizens. Here organised labour has a crucial rôle. It has been estimated that in 1964 when the percentage increase in the total African wage bill was 26·4 that there would have been a possible increase of 49,800 jobs if the increase in average earnings had been limited to the increase in productivity, say about three per cent. Instead in that year average earnings rose by 19·4 per cent and the actual increase in employment was of the order of 13,000. One of the objectives of the First National Development Plan is to increase employment by 100,000 jobs. "It should also be stressed that this objective of 400,000 in 1970 depends on the achievement of the output targets . . . and on increases in real wages and salaries not significantly greater than five per cent per annum for the low income group and three per cent per annum for the high income group" (*First National Development Plan*, July 1966, p. 7). On page 74 the Plan notes that the target of 100,000 extra jobs will be achieved only if "there is no accelerated trend towards more mechanised methods of production, which substitute machines for men". This in turn we are told requires that "increases in wages, incomes and profits are kept in line with national economic interests and not dictated by the individual interests of any single group of employers or employees" (*ibid.*). In July of this year the Vice-President, Mr. S. Kapwepwe, appealed for a freeze on wage increases for two years. If the unions accept his appeal it will be a big step forward in slowing down the growth of capital intensive methods of production.

Even if the Development Plan's target of 100,000 extra jobs is realised there will still be thousands without the possibility of obtaining paid employment. For example, during the four years of the Plan between 185–190,000 persons will leave the educational system. So between 85–90,000 will not find paid employment; their future must be either unemployment or self-employment. Apart from the waste of the previous expenditure on education Zambia cannot allow them to rot in unemployment. They are human beings and a system that would tolerate such a tragedy on the plea that this is the necessary condition of progress would stand condemned as subordinating people to things—the antithesis of Humanism. The only remedy consonant with Humanism is to enable them to become self-employed on the land. Hence for a double reason—(i) to lessen the gap in income between subsistence farmers and the rest of the community, and (ii) to afford so many young persons the possibility of making a respectable livelihood—society is morally obliged to give those in agriculture a special opportunity. As agriculture and Humanism is the subject of a special study I do not propose to say any more about it. All the other members of society—employers and employed, manual and clerical workers —must be ready to make the necessary sacrifices to make agriculture a rewarding way of life. They should not look on the aid given to rural dwellers as a form of free handout or pampering that has been taken from their hard-won earnings. Society can allow them to make their high earnings in industry only if it is ready to help those for whom there is no room in industry. Humanism demands that the "haves" make sacrifices for the "have-nots". The emphasis given to agriculture in the Plan has been fully borne out by the President's speech at Mulungushi, 19th April, 1968.

Primacy of work

Up to this point we have considered some of the main differences between the money and subsistence economies. But there is one basic point that has not changed, namely the primacy of work. It is still the source of the national income even though it may have acquired the more aseptic name "productivity". Chiefly as a result of some of the factors that earlier influenced trade union action, but due also to the shortage of skilled supervisors and the inexperience of many of the newly promoted Zambians, discipline and productivity declined in recent years. The position was aggravated by the short-

ages of semi-skilled and skilled workers who were able to use the
fact to avoid sanctions for indiscipline and absenteeism. Productivity fell seriously in building and construction. A rash of wild-
cat strikes occurred in road transport, railways, local government.
Recently, however, the government has become anxious about
indiscipline and low productivity. Government ministers call
repeatedly for hard work. Seminars on productivity have been
instituted particularly on the Copperbelt. These seem to have led
to a big improvement because Rhodesia Selection Trust reported a
notable increase in productivity in the past few months. Government
action against wild-cat strikes has hardened recently. A rail strike was
declared illegal and the army and police were called out when the Vice-
President ordered Lusaka municipal workers to return to work
within 24 hours. Some trade union leaders seem reluctant to discipline their members but the general secretary of the Zambia
Congress of Trade Unions, Mr. Wilson Chakulya, has been very
outspoken against illegal strikes. The President, Dr. Kaunda, re-
iterating a request of the Vice-President, has hinted at a wage-freeze
for three to four years.

Rôle of Trade Unions in the new Zambia

That these actions by workers are against Humanism and mutual
aid is self-evident. But if trade unions cannot press for higher
wages and better working conditions what is their rôle in the new
Zambia? There must be shift in emphasis from wage rates to
productivity, greater worker education and training, attention to
safety and health of workers. Perhaps the most urgent need is for
the unions to deal promptly and efficiently with day-to-day grievances
on the shop floor. These if allowed to fester can erupt in irresponsible
action by the workers. There has been a number of fairly serious
strikes concerning which the union leaders professed to know very
little. Better and more rapid contact between union officials and
workers in the factory or workshop must be organised immediately.

Employers can help in this reshaping of union activity by having
more frequent formal and informal contacts with unions, looking
on them more as co-operators than as an emergency squad to
discipline workers. All of this presupposes that a real effort is made
to improve what has been called "human relations in industry".
A start could be made by the employers' organisations and the
Zambia Congress of Trade Unions setting up a joint working

group to spell out in detail methods of carrying out the conclusions and recommendations of the Livingstone Labour Conference, April 1967 under the heading of: Improvements in the channels of communications between employers' and employees' organisations and between those organisations and the Government.

Recommendations for better communication between employers and workers

This committee felt that in certain cases there is inadequate consultation between employers and employees and it was therefore of the opinion that the following recommendations should be given consideration:

(i) That as far as possible Works Committees should be established in all places of work. It is important that these Works Committees must be made effective at all levels if they are going to provide the type of consultation which this Committee envisages. The main purpose of the Works Committee should be to form the communication between the workers and the management. The Committee also felt that Works Committees should have a definite form of terms of reference and procedures which should be made clear to all workers and the management. In addition to regular meetings of the Works Committee there should be occasional informal consultations between the parties concerned where this is necessary. It was also agreed that the workers' representatives on these Works Committees should be elected by the workers to cater for all grades and types of work.

(ii) Communications, to be effective, must be continuous and for this purpose it is necessary to have a flow of information from top management to the workers through line management and, similarly, communications upwards from the shop floor to top management. This can only be achieved if all supervisors and Trade Union representatives are trained in order to meet this requirement. Employers should therefore take active steps to ensure that all supervisors are trained in man-management and industrial relations and the trade unions, with Government encouragement, should take active steps to train shop stewards in all aspects of their duties. It is noted that the key point of all communications is at the level of the first-line supervisor and those working for him. A useful pattern can be obtained from the Leggett Plan.

(iii) The Committee believes that the communications at top level, i.e. between top management and the head offices of the trade unions are generally satisfactory.

(iv) It is noted by the Committee that the National Labour Consultative Council, which is a tripartite organisation at national level, has not been used quite effectively for some time past. The Committee recommends that this form of communication between employers' and employees' organisations and Government should be strengthened in order to provide an even flow of ideas between all the parties concerned. It is also felt that in addition to the National Labour Consultative Council there should be formed District Labour Consultative Councils on the same principles to discuss matters of mutual interest at the district level and there should be some form of co-ordination between the District Labour Consultative Councils and the National Labour Consultative Council.

Our system of settling disputes

It was generally agreed that our present machinery for settling disputes as laid down in the Industrial Conciliation Act was quite adequate.

But whereas the committee felt that this present machinery was quite adequate, it noted that grievances and disputes procedure in certain industries were not adequate. It was further felt that where employees are effectively organised, the employers' and employees' organisations should draw up a procedure which must be adhered to. On the other hand, where employees are not effectively organised, the Government should draw up standards of procedure to be followed.

Strikes

The committee recognised that there were two forms of strike. One is the spontaneous strike which usually occurs when something is radically wrong with industrial relations in the industry concerned. This indicates a lack of good will between workers and management and this should not happen if the recommendations and observations which have been made in relation to communications and disputes procedures are implemented wholeheartedly.

The second kind of strike is the organised strike which usually takes place when communications between employers and employees are bad. It is also noted that this type of strike can take place when there is a breakdown in negotiations or mishandling of disputes at the higher level.

The committee noted that the following constitute some of the major causes of strikes:

(i) Inadequate remuneration.
(ii) Bad management methods.
(iii) Lack of collective bargaining machinery.
(iv) Lack of good will and co-operation between management and employees' representatives.
(v) Attitudes of employers and employees to industrial problems.
(vi) Lack of sense of security and belonging among the work-people.
(vii) Lack of effective trade union organisation.
(viii) Incompetence of some supervisors to supervise properly.

The committee recommends the following solutions to some of the problems that cause strikes:

(i) The remnants of racial mistrust must be eliminated.
(ii) Disputes and grievances procedures must be followed in the event of the development of disputes.
(iii) There must be good communications between employers and employees.
(iv) An atmosphere must be created where the work-people feel a sense of belonging and security.
(v) Persons who are placed in supervisory positions must be given the necessary training and equipment to enable them to supervise properly.
(vi) There must be a programme to educate workers in their responsibilities not only to their employers but to the nation as a whole.

For the unity of the nation a more balanced appreciation of the value of every kind of work is required. Owing to past history the ideal form of work and the only form suitable for a person with education was a white-collar job, preferably in a town office. This outlook on work is by now almost instinctive. So to take up a trade or craft is beneath an educated man's status, while agriculture is "dirty work suitable only for ignorant peasants". Until this utterly erroneous concept of work is banished from the minds of Zambians there will be a reluctance to take up crafts and agriculture will stagnate. All work is ennobled by being done by a human person, all work is a service to others. The carrying out of Humanism requires the *work* of all the population. It will not be done by speeches and writing. It can be done only by the constant hard work of men trying to act in a modern society under the ideals of the Zambian past.

8

THE NEW ECONOMIC POLICY

—Implications for the Banking and Monetary Sectors*

N. A. Mujumdar†

The new economic policy outlined by His Excellency the President in his Mulungushi speech on the 19th April, 1968, has several important implications for the banking and monetary sectors. The purpose of this article is to spell out these implications and also to sketch the outlines of the new shape which the monetary policy might take in the future years. Of course, this article is more in the nature of an exploration of the various possibilities that the new economic measures throw open, rather than an exposition of official policy. These implications can be conveniently discussed under three separate sections, namely the banking and the monetary sectors, and the exchange control operations.

I The banking sector
The background

An important aspect of the President's speech was the emphasis on the fact that the commercial banks and other financial institutions in the country have not shown any particular keenness to assist Zambian businessmen. To appreciate the significance of this point it is necessary to view the problem against the broader background of an economy in which the dominance of expatriates in business and trade was being buttressed by a banking system which itself is supra-territorial in character. Some background facts about the banking system would be in order at this stage.

---

*I wish to thank Dr. J. B. Zulu, Governor, Bank of Zambia, for permitting me to publish this article.

†DR. N. A. MUJUMDAR, Director of Research, Bank of Zambia, is on secondment from the Reserve Bank of India. He was a Nuffield Fellow at the Oxford University in 1959. His publications include, besides numerous research papers, two books: *Some problems of Underemployment*, published by the Bombay University; and *Agricultural Economic Theory and the Indian Economy*, which he wrote jointly with Prof. J. R. Bellerby of Oxford University.

There are four commercial banks operating in Zambia, all of which are foreign-owned. Three of these have their head offices outside Zambia, while one is incorporated in Zambia. Development of the banking system has been one of the important elements in Zambia's economic growth since Independence. This is evident in the rate of growth of deposits; total deposits which stood at about K91 million towards the end of 1965 exceeded K140 million by the end of 1967, thus recording a rise of 54 per cent over the two-year period (see Table 1 below). This consistent up-trend in deposits growth reflects not only the widening but also the deepening of the banking system in the country. The widening of the banking system is reflected in the rate at which branch expansion has proceeded during the last two years; at present the commercial banks operate 51 branches, in addition to ten sub-branches and 69 agencies.

TABLE 1

Commercial banks—selected indicators (in millions of kwacha)

Item	1965		1966		1967	
	June	December	June	December	June	December
	K	K	K	K	K	K
1. Reserves	10·66	14·42	14·04	13·26	12·34	15·25
(a) Notes and coins	2·60	5·06	3·16	4·38	3·04	4·80
(b) Balances with the Bank of Zambia ..	8·06	9·36	10·88	8·88	9·30	10·45
2. Foreign Assets ..	13·16	9·52	17·12	13·22	2·32	12·94
(a) Balances with banks abroad	13·08	9·44	17·06	13·14	2·24	12·86
(b) Foreign Notes and Coins	0·08	0·08	0·06	0·08	0·08	0·08
3. Claims on Government	18·94	20·66	23·12	21·78	13·42	13·72
(a) Treasury Bills	9·62	11·12	13·84	11·92	3·40	5·22
(b) Investment in Government	9·32	9·54	9·28	9·86	10·02	8·50
4. Claims on Private Sector	32·66	40·70	44·10	66·22	87·60	91·88
(a) Loans and advances ..	26·24	32·44	33·14	38·44	50·80	67·46
(b) Bills of Exchange	6·42	8·26	10·96	27·78	36·80	24·42
5. Total Deposits ..	81·54	91·50	105·52	120·36	125·32	141·04
(a) Demand Deposits	52·06	64·00	72·24	85·00	82·52	96·60
(b) Time and Savings Deposits ..	29·48	27·50	33·28	35·36	42·80	44·44

Moreover, the growth in deposits is in part also attributable to the fact that the wage-paid sections of the Zambian population are being increasingly brought into the fold of the banking system.

Credit to the Zambian sector—special problems

While thus the commercial banks seem to have played an important role in mobilising savings, it is difficult to say whether Zambian enterprises have actually benefited to any great extent from the resources of the banking sector. This is partly because the expatriate businesses have evidenced substantial expansion as part of the post-Independence economic boom. It was therefore much easier for the commercial banks to channel their credit mainly to expatriate businesses which had established firm roots in the economy, rather than go out of the way seeking Zambian businessmen who had potentialities of development. Extending credit to the expatriate sector of the economy did not warrant any departure from the conventional framework within which the commercial banks are accustomed to operate. On the other hand, the picture was different with respect to the Zambian sector. The small and the medium trader, the new and struggling *entrepreneur*, the small farmer who is crossing the subsistence stage—all these categories of Zambians probably stood largely precluded from the banking sector. The process of bringing such categories of Zambians into the fold of the banking system requires a twofold progress: business methods and standards on the one hand, and banking techniques and practices on the other. Economic activities of this type have to be made "bankable" through, for instance, maintenance of proper accounts and greater regularity in meeting debt service obligations. At the same time, banking techniques and practices have to be adopted to take account of the requirements of these sectors. Lending on the basis of the character and integrity of the borrower, his earning power and repaying capacity rather than mere security, together with lending related to new forms of productive activity in an economy which is being diversified—these are the directions in which the banking system should have moved, if it were to meet the challenges of adequate financing of Zambian businesses and enterprises.

There was obviously little incentive for the banking system to move in these directions. Although there was substantial expansion of credit to the private sector, of about 126 per cent during the last two years (see Table 1), the growth rate of the expatriate business sector was of such an order that it seems to have absorbed the bulk of this additional credit. Though no firm figures are available, it seems reasonable to infer that hardly more than about 20 to 25 per cent of the total credit might have been claimed by the Zambian sector of the economy. Not only does it seem that the bulk of credit was claimed by the expatriate business sector, but also that an unusually large proportion of credit was channelled to the bigger-size businesses. The latter aspect is clearly brought out by an examination of the size-distribution of loans granted by banks. A striking feature of the size-distribution is the excessive concentration of loans in the K20,001 and above category; of the total advances of about K93 million granted by banks, about K84 million, or more than 90 per cent of the total, were accounted for by this category.[1] The point that is sought to be emphasised is that because it was easier for the banking system to lend to a selected number of large-scale expatriate businesses there was no particular need for the banks to ensure that the benefits of the banking sector's resources percolate to the Zambian business sector.

Implications for the new credit policy

It is against this broader perspective of the nexus between expatriate businesses and banks that the new credit policy which might now emerge has to be viewed. The President's speech envisaged the regulation of all domestic borrowing of non-Zambian individuals and enterprises. Under a directive issued by the Bank of Zambia subsequently, all applications of non-Zambian individuals or companies for grant of fresh overdraft facilities or renewal of existing overdraft facilities have now to be submitted to the Bank for prior approval.[2]

In this context is it possible to visualise the contours of the new credit policy which the Central Bank may formulate? In any case the main implications of such a policy seem to be clear enough. Broadly, one can surmise that the main objectives of the new credit policy could be:

---

1. Figures refer to April, 1968.

2. To facilitate grant of small personal loans the banks have been permitted to grant, without prior approval of the Bank of Zambia, temporary overdraft facilities up to a limit of K1,000 per individual.

(i) to discourage non-Zambian enterprises and individuals from making high profits, *mainly* with the help of domestic bank finance; this could be done in the expectation that a reduction in the availability of domestic bank finance might induce such enterprises to bring into the country funds and/or retain a relatively larger proportion of their profits, which are now being remitted abroad, for domestic use, and

(ii) to bring about a deceleration in the phenomenal rate at which money supply has been expanding during the last two years; to the extent to which it is possible to restrain further expansion of credit, this measure will have a salutary impact on the level of prices.

Easy availability of domestic bank credit has perhaps meant that there was no particular incentive for the expatriate businesses to bring into the country sizable sums from their parent companies; nor do they seem to have felt any need to plough back a considerable part of their profits into their capital. The new credit policy might be designed to correct, to the extent possible, these tendencies.

II   The monetary sector

The second possible objective brings us to a consideration of monetary factors. An outstanding feature of the monetary scene of Zambia is the phenomenal expansion in money supply which has taken place during the last two and a half years. As the figures presented in Table 2 indicate, money supply with the public has nearly doubled during the 30-month period since June 1965.[3] Both components of the money supply seem to have contributed to the expansion: while currency with the public has increased by 120 per cent demand deposits or credit to the private sector has expanded by 85 per cent. The manifestation of inflationary trends in the economy is partly attributable to this factor. Analysing these factors, the Bank has already pointed out, in its Annual Report for 1967, that taking an overall view of the situation, there seems to be need for exercise of a certain measure of monetary restraint in the coming years. One way of decelerating the rate of expansion of money supply is to restrain further expansion of credit. If the Bank therefore chooses to regulate expansion of credit, within what it considers as the permissible level, it can do so with the help of the new measure.

---

3. For a detailed discussion of this point, please see the Annual Report of the Bank of Zambia, 1967.

TABLE 2

Money supply—1965–1967 (in millions of kwacha)

Item	1965		1966		1967	
	June	*December*	*June*	*December*	*June*	*December*
Money Supply with the Public.. ..	67·92	82·56	93·78	113·36	113·46	131·72
Currency outside banks	15·86	18·56	21·54	28·36	30·94	35·12
Demand Deposits ..	52·06	64·00	72·24	85·00	82·52	96·60

While restraining the expansion of credit, however, it is necessary to ensure at the same time that the permitted credit expansion is in consonance with the priorities implicit in the national development plan. In other words, the objective of credit restraint has to be pursued by providing a degree of selectivity in the use of bank credit. As illustrative of the areas in which the rate of credit expansion may be slowed down, mention may be made of credit granted to non-Zambian enterprises in the construction and distribution sectors. Similarly, since Zambia is producing sizable surpluses of maize, there would be no harm if the size of credit to the non-Zambian farmers producing mainly maize is also contained. The idea underlying this approach is that economic activities which need to be accorded priority in the development plan, like manufacturing, or non-maize farming, should not be adversely affected by abrupt reductions in credit.

As a logical corollary of such credit restraint, one could hope that the banks would be induced, in future, to lend more and more to Zambian individuals and enterprises. Credit restraint, viewed in this context, thus becomes an instrument for diverting a part of the credit away from the non-Zambian sector to the Zambian sector.

III Exchange control operations

One of the characteristic features of the foreign-controlled companies in Zambia has been that some of them have tended to remit abroad a large proportion of their profits, rather than reinvesting them within the country. To restrain this undesirable tendency, the President's speech envisaged that henceforth such foreign-controlled enterprises will be permitted to remit profits and dividends only when these profits and dividends do not exceed 30 per cent of equity capital of the company concerned and provided further that the 30 per cent does not exceed one-half of the net profits. This restriction on remittances of profits and dividends was regarded necessary to prevent gross under-capitalisation of expatriate businesses.

IV Concluding comments

An attempt was made in this article to spell out the main implications of the new economic policy for the monetary and banking sectors. Much will no doubt depend upon what exact shape the new monetary policy will take in actuality. All that the article attempted to indicate was the various possibilities, thrown open by the new economic policy, for the Central Bank to reshape its monetary policy. For instance, the restraint on credit expansion as visualised here, if adopted as a desirable policy, might not only help in attaining the primary objective of diverting a part of the credit away from the non-Zambian sector to the Zambian sector, but will also help in containing inflationary forces. Especially with reference to the distribution sector, such credit restraint might prevent artificial inflation of prices through excessive inventory accumulation. Further, restrictions on remittance of profits is designed to promote reinvestment of sizable sums in the domestic economy. This factor, coupled with the fact that expatriate firms may be required in future to bring into the country external funds, on an increasing scale, to meet their working capital requirements, may lead to an improvement in the balance of payments situation. On the whole, if the approach to the new credit policy outlined here were to be pursued, besides serving the primary objective of diverting a part of the credit away from the non-Zambian sector to the Zambian sector, it might be possible to generate forces which would have a salutary impact on the internal price situation and the balance of payments position.

9

INVESTMENT POLICY IN ZAMBIA

Stephen H Goodman*

The problems of economic development are an extension of the problems of resource allocation to a dynamic setting. In any particular time period there are a limited amount of resources available: skilled manpower, construction capacity, natural resources, foreign exchange, labour, transport capacity, capital, *et cetera*, that may be combined into several different economic processes each with an economic and social output the value of which is determined by the implicit objectives or welfare function of the society. This allocation of resources to achieve objectives is the basis of any investment policy.

This essay considers government investment policy in Zambia both before and after Mulungushi and analyses some of the economic effects of Mulungushi. It attempts to analyse the efforts of the Zambian government in allocating resources to maximise the value of its welfare function or achieve its objectives.

Development constraints and investment criteria

Investment criteria have usually been associated with the allocation of a particular scarce resource, capital, rather than with the allocation of a bundle of scarce resources. The special importance usually attached to capital, which may be defined as the difference between income including transfers and consumption including transfers, follows in general from capital's scarcity in most developing countries and the great part its accumulation has played in the historical development process. In the case of Zambia, particularly in the first half period of the First National Development

*STEPHEN H. GOODMAN is a National Science Foundation Fellow at Yale University completing a doctoral thesis on decision-making in industrialisation in Zambia. His contribution was written while he was an Assistant Lecturer in Economics at the University of Zambia, Lusaka. Mr. Goodman has written a number of articles on African Economic Problems.

excess's

Plan, capital has not, however, been an effective constraint on development. The income received by the Government, particularly from the taxes associated with the mining and exporting of copper, has exceeded the ability of the Government to spend this income. In general, ministries have been unable to spend their annual allocations and the Government has run surpluses.

capacity, low absorption

The non-scarcity nature of capital during the first four years of development is a natural consequence of the structure of the economy. The shortages of personnel, the slow expansion in the construction sector, the difficulties of increasing or maintaining supplies, particularly as a result of Rhodesian U.D.I. and subsequent sanctions, has made capital an inoperative constraint in the Zambian economy, although it will become an increasingly operative one in the future.

The particular circumstances facing Zambia make non-comprehensive investment criteria, or criteria which do not consider the influence of all scarce factors, meaningless. Allocating resources on the basis of naive criteria such as capital/output ratios or recoupment periods will not lead to an optimum use of resources as such criteria economise only on the use of capital. Similarly, other more sophisticated criteria which concentrate on the return to capital may neglect the other important scarcities in the economy.

Comprehensive criteria which attempt to consider the scarcity of all factors are more likely to lead to efficient investment decisions. Examples of such comprehensive criteria are variations of cost-benefit analysis where the direct and indirect costs and benefits of the project are compared and evaluated. Assigning to each factor or cost its scarcity or market clearing price and assigning to each benefit its value in terms of the objectives or welfare function will permit the calculation of the net benefit associated with each project. Choosing those projects with the maximum net benefit will lead to optimal investment decisions where projects are marginal or small relative to the economy and where the assigned prices reflect the true economic relationships. Where projects are non-marginal the scarcity or shadow prices may have to be based on future projected conditions possibly derived from a programming solution. In the Zambian context the calculation of costs would involve the adjustment of at least the prices of unskilled labour, construction, and imports as their prices are not scarcity prices. Although capital is in surplus at the present time, its shadow price will still be positive as it is capable of storage or investment overseas and it may have a large positive future value. Only in the presence of a very strong time preference for present activity over future activity will an attempt be made to use all the capital available given the supply inelasticity or low supply responsiveness of other scarce factors.

First national development plan

Present Zambian investment policy theoretically has as its foundation the First National Development Plan formulated in 1966 and as amended annually by the development budget and as interpreted and amended by various policy statements. The plan enumerates eight investment objectives which may be summarised as a structural transformation of the economy away from copper and a reliance on the South, an improvement in levels of income, accommodation and their distribution, and relative stability in prices. aims

To achieve these objectives the plan envisions sectoral allocations based on the programmes prepared by the ministries concerned. Each ministry was encouraged to submit an imaginative maximum programme in the form of comprehensive project data sheets giving the necessary material inputs for the projects. The basic philosophy of plan construction was that the physical requirements of the investment programme undertaken would not exceed the physical balance of scarce resources available to the economy. The lack of sufficient experienced personnel, the inadequacy of existing data and plans, and the pressure of time made it difficult, however, to accurately complete the project data sheets. This coupled with the complexity of the balancing exercise made achievement of the goal of completing a physical balance unattainable. The Planning Office, furthermore, had no systematic technique of evaluation or overall investment criteria to which the proposals could be subjected. Even if a physical balance could be attained there could be no certainty about the optimality, from the point of view of government objectives, of such an allocation. The investment programme as embodied in the plan is therefore principally an amalgamation of the projected maximum programme of the ministries subject to a relatively arbitrary selection and cost minimisation procedure and as modified by the contingency needs following from U.D.I. and the effect of sanctions on Zambia. The major portion of investment funds and resources were directed to infrastructure, particularly roads, education, electric power, and housing, while a lesser sum was earmarked for directly productive investments.

During the initial period of the plan the absence of sufficient personnel to effect the full envisioned programmes meant that in general the programme actually undertaken was consistent and capable given the resources available. In no sense, however, was it known if the programme envisioned or undertaken was an optimum means of achieving the objectives with available resources. This lack of systematic evaluation of all alternative investment policies is not unique to Zambia nor is it *prima facie* evidence of inefficient resource allocation. Many nations, including most developing countries, particularly during the initial planning period, find it necessary to limit the thoroughness of investment evaluation. The inefficiencies in investment allocation which follow from the non-thoroughness of the evaluation are not necessarily more costly than the price of delay and securing increased information, particularly where information sources are weak, the number of good development opportunities is large, and the programme may be altered through periodic review.

Industrial investment policy

The important rôle played by Ministerial programmes in the formulation of the plan and as a basis of investment policy justifies a closer examination of the policies of a particular Ministry. For this purpose it is useful to examine the investment activities of the Ministry of Commerce, Industry and Foreign Trade. The usefulness of examining the activities of this ministry are further enhanced by the importance industrialisation plays in development strategy, by the implications of Mulungushi for its activities, and by the general success it has had in implementing its programme.

The principal tool of the Government and the ministry in developing and implementing government policy in industry is the Industrial Development Corporation of Zambia Ltd. (INDECO), a wholly government-owned limited liability company within the responsibility of the Ministry of Commerce, Industry and Foreign Trade. At the time of plan formulation INDECO, which had already been in existence for more than five years, had a group of projects, most of which had been developed since independence, which on the basis of the information then available appeared profitable in a commercial sense or were directed at a particular government objective. These projects were submitted by the ministry as the basis of their maximum programme and were accepted as the industrial portion of the plan.

In selecting projects for investigation INDECO's basic philosophy has been to choose projects with good commercial returns, but for which private capital is lacking, although some consideration has been given to foreign exchange savings, employment effects, and structural changes in the economy. In deciding which projects to investigate further the basic criterion has been the size of market as estimated from the import statistics relative to efficient plant size. If it appeared that a product, formerly imported, could be produced in Zambia with a reasonable return and with little increase in tariff protection, or if it appeared that a product vital to the diversification of the economy could be produced in Zambia with a reasonable increase in tariff protection, then a more careful investment study was generally undertaken. The danger, however, of using import statistics to identify investment opportunities for further study is that alternative export promoting investment opportunities, that may be superior, are ignored. Using import substitution as a basis of development has not either theoretically or empirically been shown to be an optimum development strategy. In the Zambian context, where the size of the domestic market is relatively small, the neglect of export activities, particularly after the few simple and profitable import substituting projects are undertaken, may be a serious error. In practice only one government industrial investment project has any export content, and this project is thought to be one of the better industrial investments.

On the basis of the initial screening more intensive investment studies were usually undertaken, frequently with the assistance of consultants and potential investment partners. The principal purpose of these studies was to judge the profitability or viability of the proposed investment in the Zambian environment and with given technologies.

The use of returns to capital or profitability as a basis of government investment allocation is likely to lead to inefficient investment decisions where the prices of other resources do not express their scarcity value in the economy. In the face of widespread unemployment among the unskilled, not reflected in their wage rate, limited expansion possibilities in construction capacity, not reflected in the price of works, and surplus capital relative to the ability of the economy to absorb it, the use of commercial profitability as an investment criterion and guide will not lead to maximum income or a maximum achievement of objectives. The unsuitability of profit as a criterion was in part recognised, but in the absence of overall guidelines and sufficient understanding of the development process it was thought more useful to make *ad-hoc* adjustments in particular circumstances rather than introduce possibly incorrect price adjustments.

The industrial investment policy as embodied in the plan therefore represents a perception of opportunities at a particular period of time judged primarily on a commercial basis. In general with changes in circumstances the perception has changed and new programmes have been added or old ones deleted. It is interesting to note in this regard, however, that few projects once carried as far as an investment study are rejected, which either speaks highly of the initial screening process or questions the efficacy of the ultimate selection procedure.

Foreign investors

Prior to independence in 1964 foreign investment (including mining investment) constituted well over one-half of total investment. During the period of the plan, it is believed that although private investment will amount to only 34.3 per cent of total investment the absolute amount of such investment will increase. The importance of foreign investment and the expertise with which it is associated is much greater than its financial contribution, particularly in Zambia where entrepreneurial ability and skilled manpower are in short supply.

The theoretical demarcation between state and private sectors or between areas for government and private investment, at least prior to Mulungushi, was indicated in the Government's statement on industrial development of April 1965. Iron and steel, fertilizer, arms, ammunition and explosives, and other industries of major importance or which were basic to the economy, were reserved for government control. All other industries could be privately or jointly controlled. In practice it usually has been considered desirable on the part of large private investors to invite government participation in their enterprise as a sign of goodwill, while the government in promoting industrial projects has almost always sought to enlist foreign expertise through management or consultancy agreements where the managing party is given an interest in the success of the enterprise through an equity ownership. Where the theoretical demarcation of the industrial policy statement differed from the alternatives actually available at the time the project was advanced, the policy statement demarcation was in general neglected. This point is well illustrated in the case of explosives where control was placed in the hands of the private promoters, who in any case would be subject to government control and influence, despite the clear statement that this should be a government enterprise.

In implementing and initating investment policy, particularly in industry, the Government frequently finds itself affected by the activities of the potential foreign investor. For large projects in developing countries the three primary sources of foreign investment and expertise are what I shall call machinery merchants, technical merchants and expatriate marketers. Machinery merchants have throughout Africa and the developing world shown an eagerness actively to promote uneconomic as well as economic projects in which the profits on the sale of machinery and the technical fees received assure them of adequate returns regardless of the outcome of the project itself. The experience with projects promoted by such merchants has sometimes been unfavourable, but their extremely active salesmanship, frequently directed at politically if not economically viable projects, and sometimes assisted by the activities of their home governments or allied consulting institutes, have assured them of continuing sales.

The technical merchant is eager to encourage activities which can make use of his expertise and commercial experience. In most cases willing to participate in the equity of the firm, and willing to purchase machinery through competitive tender, his profits are limited to his fee and his equity return, which are both usually linked to the profitability of the enterprise. The unfortunate tendency, however, of developing countries to judge the performance of the enterprise by commercial criteria, even when prices do not reflect economic reality, and the additional tendency to protect the profit of inefficient enterprises through higher tariffs, often results in inefficiently operated plants which do not make optimum use of the resource combination available. The rôle of the machinery or technical merchant has been a relatively small one in Zambia, but it does exist.

The other principal source of foreign capital or expertise, the expatriate marketer, is usually a reluctant investor. The expatriate marketer already sells his product in the domestic market and seeks only to protect his market share. He will usually try to postpone an investment as long as possible, preferring to continue satisfying the demand from the output of existing plants elsewhere. Only when his market position is threatened by actual or potential government action aimed at import substitution and the market is in fact large enough for a relatively efficient plant will the expatriate marketer actually invest. In such cases, he will usually prove, because of his technical and sales knowledge, a useful investor. Such projects have generally shown reasonable commercial returns.

Private investment, other than by machinery or technical merchants and expatriate marketers, tends to be almost non-existent in most developing economies. Although it is an important source of commercial and technical ability the small expatriate business is an insignificant source of foreign capital. In Zambia the expatriate has played an especially important rôle because of the weaknesses of the Zambian entrepreneurial class, but the unwillingness of both the Government and the business community to effect a dialogue based on mutual advantage, and the general distrust felt by both parties, has meant that much of this expatriate talent is directed at short-range, quick profit schemes.

An additional source of foreign capital and expertise in Zambia are the mining companies. Capital expenditures by the two mining companies approximated K30 million annually prior to Mulungushi with the bulk of this investment being spent in the mining sector, although the Anglo-American Corporation has undertaken some non-mining ventures. This investment is generally commercially motivated and is responsive to expected returns. It is likely that the size of this investment would have been significantly larger were the mining companies more certain of their future rôle and had the tax structure been more sensibly based.

In joint enterprises with foreign investors and in managing its own directly productive enterprises government policy has in general been to avoid interfering in the day-to-day operations and management of establishments. Government control is exercised through periodic board meetings and reviews of accounts rather than through direct civil service administration. This policy has the advantage that enterprises are not subjected to political interference or indecisive management. It has the disadvantage, however, that many of the government's non-commercial objectives, which may justify the investment, will be unrealised.

Government controlled or jointly owned enterprises have not in general redirected their imports to suppliers or routes more compatible with government policy and objectives except where required by regulations which have been made applicable to all companies. Government enterprises are frequently managed by agents or companies possessing South African or Rhodesian residence and employment policies have frequently not been reorientated. In some cases government enterprises have used their special influence in government to have import and employment regulations waived for their benefit. The independence of control present in government enterprises and the reliance on profitability as a criterion of good management may result in the non-achievement by government enterprises of the Government's non-commercial objectives.

Before Mulungushi

Prior to Mulungushi government investment policy was not necessarily optimum from the point of view of government objectives. Investments were undertaken in line with a programme which took no account of the operative restraints, and provided for no comparison between the returns on different sectoral investments. The neglect of the important physical bottlenecks existing in Zambia implicit in allocating investments on a financial basis made it difficult to undertake physically all planned programmes and achieve all objectives. An attempt to raise government investment from an annual level of approximately K36 million per annum in the period 1954–1964 to a level of K140 million per annum during the plan period, in the face of increasing private investments, shortages of manpower, and shortages of supplies, had as its natural consequence a rapid increase in prices which may permit plan fulfilment in financial terms but not in real terms. In such circumstances investment allocations of capital, and investment decisions based on returns to capital, usually unadjusted, cannot lead to the most correct allocation of the limited real resources available.

The nature of the planning and implementation process favours the undertaking of programmes which will employ financial resources without regard to achievements. In the first half of the plan period the projects most successfully implemented, with the exception of contingency projects, have generally been the large-scale projects least associated with the structural change envisioned as an objective of the plan. The principal structural alterations envisioned and emphasised in the plan: increased employment, development of rural areas, a Zambianisation of economic life, decreased dependence on copper, *et cetera*, were in general not realised despite the fact that financial expenditures neared planned levels, the government faced deficits, and foreign exchange difficulties were expected.

After Mulungushi

The Mulungushi statement represents a watershed in government investment policy in Zambia. Although it is premature to evaluate the implications of the statement it is still possible to note the changes that are taking place in investment policy as Zambia moves from a capital surplus to a capital shortage economy and as some of the physical bottlenecks are overcome.

The new realities of the Zambian economy—the presence of a government deficit on capital account, a potential deficit on current foreign exchange transactions, a realisation of the difficulties of achieving the desired structural transformations—has prompted more careful thinking on priorities and allocations. The advantage of being poor and knowing it, particularly in Zambia where physical bottlenecks are still important, is that it encourages a more careful use of financial and, therefore, other resources.

As a result of new stringencies attempts are being made to introduce comprehensive investment criteria which will take account of the scarcity relationships of the economy and the structural objectives. Initial work is being undertaken on a standard cost-benefit technique that would be both simple to apply and reasonably reflective of the real economic conditions. Particular attention will be directed to the labour and import components of projects, with the cost of labour being adjusted to reflect the difference between the money wage and the social value and cost of employing labour, and with the cost of imports being adjusted to the import price less duties possibly adjusted for foreign exchange deficiencies. These new more comprehensive criteria which it is hoped to apply to all projects considered for the second plan will permit a more efficient allocation of investment funds and other scarce resources between and within sections.

It is expected that more attention will be given to the smaller projects which may make less use of scarce resources but which affect many of the non-income or structural objectives of government policy as emphasised in Mulungushi. As examples, increased emphasis is being placed on the development of small-scale mines, the maintenance of employment, particularly in Barotse province, the development of nursery estates of small Zambian-owned craft or service facilities, and the provision of advisory services and additional loan finance to small Zambian entrepreneurs and co-operatives. Although many of these projects are still far from realisation their economic, political and humanitarian importance is increasingly realised.

In its new investments in twenty-five companies, to be administered by INDECO, probably the least important aspect of Mulungushi, the Government expects to exert influence on prices and profits in the building supply industry, rationalise transport, share in the excessive brewery profits and maintain employment in Barotse. The general effect, given the nature of the Zambian economy with its supply inelasticities, will probably be to shift part of the excessive profits to Government rather than reducing prices or inducing rationalisation or structural change. The total size of these twenty-five investments will be small, about K10 million, but the commercial returns and in a few cases potential structural returns should be large, The danger, however, is that the companies will be administered as they have been in the past, with the emphasis being placed on profitability rather than Zambianisation, low prices and increased employment as a criterion of good management. If this is to be the case, the result could more easily and less dramatically have been achieved through higher taxation.

Probably the most economically significant part of Mulungushi, the restrictions on profit repatriation, will have little effect on government investment policy. Joint government–private (foreign) investment projects will be little affected although some potential private investors may now expect greater government participation. Projects financed exclusively by private investment will above a certain investment level become less numerous but such projects have always, outside of the mines, been insignificant. Mulungushi has probably not greatly affected the confidence of the large investor. He in many cases, particularly since Arusha, has already discounted his return by factors to reflect potential nationalisation or profit repatriation restrictions. The private investor, the machinery or technical merchant or expatriate marketer, has in the past usually relied on and secured formal agreements with the Government, the contents of which have not been affected at all by Mulungushi. The machinery merchant in any case earns his returns on his sales, while the expatriate marketer will still seek to protect his market position as long as the return he may remit including management fees is reasonable—which in most cases it is—and he has the good-will and consent or protection of the government. The small foreign investor may be deterred by Mulungushi but in terms of capital flows he has always been insignificant, preferring to finance from suppliers' credits, profits and overdrafts. Mulungushi may delay some investment as private investors wait for the promised invest-ment guarantee certificates and a clarification of their rôle, or nego-tiate with government on the extent of equity and the management fee for their expertise but the overall effect, with the possible exception of the mines, will be small. Some small amount of government investment funds will have to be made available, however, for the expansion of government trading in the rural areas, and for the provision of increased loan funds for Zambian entrepreneurs.

The big question mark with regard to Mulungushi and govern-ment investment policy is the reaction of the two great mining firms. Harry Oppenheimer for Anglo-American Corporation and Sir Ronald Prain for Roan Selection Trust have already expressed their dislike of the profit repatriation provisions. What they will do, however, with their new-found liquidity is uncertain. Whether they will use it to replace new mining investments from other sources overseas, to expand their real investments in Zambia, or to acquire financial assets no one is sure, nor has consideration been given to the compatibility of increased investments by these firms with the desire for greater Zambian control of the economy. But in terms of the size of capital flows their reaction is of some importance.

In summary it is too early to be sure of all the implications of Mulungushi but in terms of investment policy we can probably look forward to more rational investment allocations by govern-ment, slightly reduced private investments from the non-mining firms, and an increase in the investments, particularly in financial assets, by the two great mining companies.

10

A PLEA FOR UNDERSTANDING*

His Excellency Dr K D Kaunda
President of the Republic of Zambia

A great deal has been said and written about the economic reforms I announced at Mulungushi in Zambia on 19th April, 1968. I regret to say that most of it displays ignorance of the conditions prevailing in my country.

In fact I feel that the cause of the mistrust and misunderstanding between developed and developing nations is due to this ignorance and the very lack of appreciation by the former of the problems facing the latter. This is the reason why every step taken by a developing country towards achievement of a national economic identity and independence is scrutinised, interpreted and misinterpreted by the developed world.

The conclusions invariably attribute racial motives to the reforms or try to identify the reforms with known economic theories which developed in Europe during the last few decades. They usually end up by describing the policies of the country as being pro-West or pro-East. I do feel very strongly about this and I feel that it is time that actions taken by developing countries are examined in the light of circumstance prevailing in the countries themselves and in the light of the needs of the countries to set up their own course towards their economic independence.

I must spend a little time explaining some of the economic problems facing my nation in order to enable you to appreciate the reasoning behind Zambia's recent economic reforms. Zambia achieved Independence on the 24th October, 1964. At that time the people of Zambia took over political control, but the economy was dominated entirely by foreign and resident expatriate business.

How this came about does not need going into at this particular

*Address to the Overseas Development Institute, London, on 18th July, 1968

moment. All I need to say is that when Zambia achieved independence all these foreign and resident expatriate businesses were operated by foreign and expatriate people. No Zambians had been given the opportunity to make a career in business. No Zambians could be found in jobs above those of unskilled and semi-skilled workers in industry.

It was obvious that during the time of the Federation the expatriate businessmen had chosen to create a closed shop very much like the European Mine Workers Union of Northern Rhodesia which had an agreement with the mining companies that only white people could be employed in certain jobs on the mines. On independence, therefore, you will see that we had to cope with a business community foreign-owned and foreign-managed.

We spent a great deal of time pleading with the business community and pointing out to them that it was in their best interest to introduce Zambians into management jobs. We received plenty of promises but very little action. In addition to the pleas to train Zambians as managers we tried to help the few Zambian businessmen develop by assisting them with loans.

However, you do realise the amount of money needed to develop out of nothing Zambian business to a level comparable with expatriate business. It would be impossible for the Government to provide sufficient funds for this purpose and loan schemes were scratching the surface of the problem only.

In the meantime, we had embarked upon the implementation of the transitional and first national development plan which created unprecedented boom conditions in the country. Despite their previous pessimistic predictions, businessmen found themselves in a profits paradise after Independence. The activity which was generated as a result of government spending was unheard of in the past.

We had plenty of needs. We needed schools, we needed hospitals, we needed roads and we set about to build them as fast as possible. The business community set about collecting the profits which resulted out of this fantastic boom and spent even less time in worrying about promoting a Zambian in business.

On top of this, Rhodesia declared Independence unilaterally which imposed upon us the need for even more government spending in order to create new import routes and alleviate problems created by the new situation. The result was that when our demands were highest our ability to bring supplies in was curtailed. The businessmen again took advantage of the situation.

Both my ministers and I spent a great deal of time pointing out to the business community their short-sightedness and the dangers inherent in their actions. In January 1967, addressing the National Development Conference in Kitwe, I said this:

> "Government is much disturbed over certain trends in industry which reflect anything but a concern for productivity. Some sectors of industry (and commerce) are taking deliberate advantage of the transportation and economic problems besetting this country for their own private gain. There is increasing evidence of grossly inflated mark-ups, inflated beyond any level justified by transportation costs of distribution in Zambia.
>
> The Government is increasingly concerned over the dangers implied in this trend, and determined not to let it go unchecked . . .
>
> I find it amazing that businessmen, who appear to hold the free price system in such high regard, can at the same time consciously and deliberately contribute with such effectiveness to its destruction.
>
> For that is precisely what the mark-up marauders are doing. They are simply inviting Government—*and soon they may find they have forced Government*—to move in with compulsory checks upon the free price system, or to go even further and replace it altogether in some sectors of the economy.
>
> Zambia would be by no means the first country in which such action has been forced upon an unwilling Government. And if it does happen, who will be the first to cry but those who, by their own greed, their own determination to take advantage of a difficult and unfortunate situation, left the Government no choice but to act?"

Business, however, did not respond. On the contrary, profit margins increased even higher and we have evidence of large-scale exchange control evasion by illegal means. It was obvious to us, therefore, that the members of the business community in Zambia who had chosen, despite our many appeals, not to take up Zambian nationality were there to make hay while the sun shines, and if rain comes, to run for shelter in their home countries. The need, therefore, to Zambianise business became imperative.

If our appeals to promote Zambians into management executive posts to run the affairs of foreign business had failed, if our loan schemes to help the advancement of Zambian business were slow, it was obvious that some new and more drastic approach should be adopted.

At Mulungushi on the 19th April, 1968, I directed that from the 1st January, 1969, trade and contracting should be confined to Zambians. I consider these two fields as being the less sophisticated business areas and ones in which Zambians could quickly develop if they are protected against competition by expatriates. As from 1st January, 1969, trading by non-Zambians will be confined to the centres of ten large towns of the country. In all other areas only Zambians or State-controlled organisations will have the right to trade. Similarly contracting and quarrying has been confined to Zambians. I am confident that in these two fields Zambian business will take root, and I look forward to the day when people who have succeeded in those fields will move to the more sophisticated fields of business such as industry and finance.

When this happens we will truly have achieved economic independence in that we will have achieved a national economic identity. When this happens, we shall not be judged as to whether our methods of business are Western or Eastern, capitalist or communist. When this happens, our methods will be simply Zambian.

I consider this as the first essential step in the implementation of the philosophy of Humanism, because I feel that the Zambian businessmen will agree to operate within the framework of this social philosophy which is entirely Zambian and which therefore they understand by instinct. As I indicated during my announcement of the reforms, it is my intention to encourage private initiative in Zambia. I want Zambian businessmen to develop so that they can be of service to their fellow human beings. In other words, I do not want them to get rich at the expense of the rest of the nation. Exploitation, whether it is done by people of one racial group against another or done by people of the same racial group against their own kith and kin, is wrong, and we will not glorify it in Zambia by allowing it a place. We are fiercely determined to fight it wherever it shows its ugly head. Even as I say this, I know that this is not an easy thing to fight.

Let me emphasise that I want Zambian businesses to expand and to prosper. But for goodness sake, I do not propose to create Zambian capitalism. This is incompatible with my conception of Humanism. I want to see the co-operative spirit develop. I want to see the businesses operate as co-operatives or as companies rather than as individuals. If they operate as companies I want to see that when they have achieved success they will give the opportunity to their fellow Zambians to share their profits. When the time comes, I shall set the limits of the Zambian enterprise that can remain a purely private enterprise. These limits will be based on the amount of capital employed, on turnover and on the number of employees. When an enterprise grows beyond these limits, then it must become a public company. When it grows even further, it will be taken over by the State. We do not propose to make of Zambians business barons now or in future. In Zambia, every Zambian's contribution must ultimately be for the benefit of MAN through the State.

Another aspect of the Mulungushi reforms again designed to assist the development of Zambian enterprise is the limiting of local borrowing by resident and expatriate enterprises. Foreign business was subject to exchange control regulations and its borrowing in Zambia was regulated according to the amount brought in from abroad. Resident expatriate business was considered local and its borrowing was unlimited.

If, however, the resident expatriate business has chosen to remain expatriate four years after Independence; if its shareholders and directors have not taken up Zambian citizenship after four years of Independence, how can it expect to be treated differently than foreign companies? Besides, we are convinced that one of the reasons of exchange control evasion has been the unlimited borrowing for resident expatriate business.

In this way, companies have been kept under-capitalised, while private purses filled up, and private individuals kept busy finding illegal ways of sending money out of the country. The new regulations will go a long way to force people to capitalise their businesses properly. At the same time, it will create liquidity with which we hope banks and financial institutions will finance the emerging Zambian business.

The measure that was most widely reported in the foreign press was my request to 25 companies to offer controlling shares to the State. I would like to make it clear that these companies have been carefully selected in order to fit in the overall economic programme announced at Mulungushi.

Some of them, such as the trading companies, will assist us in providing the service in areas where the Zambian businessman is not as yet able to provide it. At the same time they would be used as the yardstick for the performance of the Zambian businessmen, and as the regulator of prices in order to prevent exploitation of the general public.

In all the cases involving trading companies, we feel, and this has been appreciated by their own directors, that the minority shareholders will be even better off in their 49 per cent ownership than they were when they owned 100 per cent. Turnover will increase substantially in view of the elimination of competition and with the increased turnovers, the profits of these companies will rise.

Other companies such as the transport companies were necessary in view of the importance of transportation in our country at the moment. You all know that the worst effect of U.D.I. has been the effect on our import capacity.

It is absolutely vital that we rationalise the transport system in order to avoid unnecessary duplication of very expensive facilities. I am, therefore, pleased to say that the two major transport companies involved have been extremely co-operative.

In the case of building materials, it was necessary that the State should have control in order to check price inflation. Some of the firms we took over were suspected of profiteering and in fact examination of their affairs after takeover has proved us to be correct.

You will not believe it when I tell you that net profits, and I repeat *net profits*, of some firms taken over amounted to between 25 and 30 per cent of turnover—and I repeat, *between 25 and 30 per cent of turnover*. Dividends were often 100 per cent and 150 per cent of capital. Of course, there have been firms which have been making losses but closer examination of their affairs revealed that when the Zambian company was making a slight loss, the parent company was enjoying administration fees as high as ten per cent.

In this way our Inland Revenue was deprived of the taxation which went to the country of origin of the company.

However, I am only mentioning this in order to indicate to you the magnitude of our problem.

I am glad to say that all firms have responded promptly and favourably to my request and negotiations have already been completed to the satisfaction of both the shareholders and my Government. We are now looking forward to many years of association and reasonable profits with our new partners.

One of the last measures of Mulungushi was the limitation of the remittance of profits to foreign shareholders. This has aroused to my surprise a great deal of adverse comment, much more than the action of the South African Government a few years back to block all foreign capital in South Africa.

This I hope has not given the impression that we are turning our backs to foreign investment. On the contrary, we welcome it and at Mulungushi I announced the proposed enactment of legislation which will guarantee to approved foreign investment "that due dividends and interest payments on foreign capital may be remitted abroad; that repatriation of capital brought in from abroad will be allowed; that no expropriation will occur for a set number of years; that any nationalisation thereafter will be at a fair valuation, the method of which shall be laid down in the certificate".

Mr. Chairman, unfortunately in this cruel world, young countries, particularly African countries, can never be right in whatever they do. If they fail to take adequate measures to develop their countries, if they fail to make a co-ordinated attack on ignorance, disease and poverty they are ridiculed and their failure is attributed to inexperience. Even worse words are used to describe their failures.

If they take measures such as we have done in Zambia in order to correct the situation and give greater force behind development in order to meet the requirements of their people they are condemned as being ignorant, impulsive, unrealistic, unscientific, etc. Indeed, we may not come out of our countries even on a planned trip.

If we do, such as I have done, for constructive purposes, it is said that it is because we are running away from our problems at home. If we don't move out of our countries it is said that it is because we fear there will be coups in our absence. When can we be right, I ask? Yet there are others in the developed world who have mountains and mountains of problems, and where efforts to solve them are not always the best.

Their failures, however, are not ridiculed and their measures are not a result of ignorance.

For young developing countries who have nothing to defend except truth, this trend, this prejudice and cynicism would have been laughable if they did not manifest a tragedy in human affairs.

. . . I hope that my exposition will contribute towards a better understanding not only between my country and the United Kingdom, but also between the developed and developing countries.

First published in 1969 by the East African Publishing House, PO Box 30571, Uniafric House, Koinange Street, Nairobi, Kenya. Made and Printed in Africa by Printing and Packaging Corporation Ltd, PO Box 30157, Nairobi, Kenya